# PRAISE FOR *ENERGIZED ENTERPRISE*

"If you're looking for a way to motivate people and energize your organization, the stories and practical examples in this book will help you do it. Dr. Marta Wilson shows how leaders can engage and fulfill the personal goals of their team members—and the goals of their organization."

—Joseph Martore, President & CEO of CALIBRE Systems, Inc.

"If you want a team that is motivated, accountable, and enthusiastic, read *Energized Enterprise*."

—Casey Coleman, Civilian Group Vice President of Unisys Federal Systems

"With Dr. Wilson's highly perceptive approach, even the most dispirited workplace can transform into a source of creativity and productivity. The principles here apply to any organization that needs to improve performance and morale. *Energized Enterprise* is a powerful tool that will ignite both hearts and minds!"

—Marshall Goldsmith, a Thinkers 50 Top Ten Global Business Thinker and
   top ranked executive coach

"As a consultant, Marta Wilson has an impressive history of helping public sector employees get results. Here she provides a public service of her own: a concise, practical leadership guide to unleashing the full potential of government employees whose talents can make a major difference in our world."

—Vice Admiral John R. Ryan, (Ret.), President and CEO of the Center
   for Creative Leadership

"Marta is unique in her ability to apply her years of leadership consulting and her passion for the subject to the issues of leadership in the public sector. She demonstrates through accessible, common-sense guidance and engaging stories that change in the public sector really does start with you."

—Ellen Glover, Executive Vice President of ICF International

"Good leaders thirst for hands-on, pragmatic approaches and steps to take that will unharness the inherent power of their workforce. While especially important in the public sector, these principles apply to any people-driven enterprise where executives are often caught in the crises of the day, and miss clear opportunities to find, attract and nurture the stars and staff who will enable their missions. I find myself re-reading key messages in *Energized Enterprise* that provide me clear pathways to inspire, develop and nurture my leaders and staff—the most important part of my job!"

—Robin Portman, Executive Vice President of Booz Allen Hamilton

"Effective leadership that challenges workforce dynamics can transform any organization. Having worked in both the Public and Private sectors, I've witnessed very different ways of becoming an effective and successful organization. Of course, there are workforce challenges in every organization and Marta Wilson gets it right in her 'Energized Enterprise.' She gives valuable insights into how common-sense organizational investments in human capital can yield big results. Her book is a fun and thought-provoking read, that can help any organization realize its full potential of performance excellence."

—Douglas Todd, Director, Government Affairs of Siemens Corporation

# ENERGIZED ENTERPRISE

Leading Your Workforce to New Peaks
of Performance in the Public Sector and Beyond

## DR. MARTA WILSON

GREENLEAF
BOOK GROUP PRESS

Published by Greenleaf Book Group Press
Austin, Texas
www.gbgpress.com

Distributed by Greenleaf Book Group

For ordering information or special discounts for bulk purchases, please contact Greenleaf Book Group at PO Box 91869, Austin, TX 78709, 512.891.6100.

For permission to reproduce copyrighted material, grateful acknowledgment is made to the following:

From "Getting New Hires Up to Speed Quickly" by Keith Rollag, Salvatore Parise and Rob Cross from *MIT Sloan Management Review*, Winter 2005. Copyright © Massachusetts Institute of Technology, 1977–2015. Reproduced by permission of the copyright holder.

From "The MRAP Vehicle Project—Project Management Institute Project of the Year Award Nomination," 2013, by David Hansen, Dennis Dean, David Gibson, and Sharon Flinder, accessed at http://www.pmi.org/learning/project-management-lives-stake-5837. Copyright © 2013 by the Project Management Institute, Inc. Reproduced by permission of the copyright holder.

From "2012 Justice and Law Enforcement Medal Recipient," from *Samuel J. Heyman Service to America Medals* website, accessed at http://servicetoamericamedals.org/SAM/recipients/profiles/jlm12_milione.shtml. Copyright © 2012 by the Partnership for Public Service. Reproduced by permission of the Partnership for Public Service, ourpublicservice.org.

From "2012 Management Excellence Medal Recipient," from *Samuel J. Heyman Service to America Medals* website, accessed at http://servicetoamericamedals.org/SAM/recipients/profiles/mem12_branch.shtml. Copyright © 2012 by the Partnership for Public Service. Reproduced by permission of the Partnership for Public Service, ourpublicservice.org.

From "Leveraging Employee Engagement for Competitive Advantage: HR's Strategic Role," by Nancy R. Lockwood from *SHRM Research Quarterly* 52.3 (2007): 1–12, accessed at http://www.shrm.org/india/hr-topics-and-strategy/employee-advocacy-relations-and-engagement/documents/07marresearchquarterly.pdf. Copyright © 2007 by Society for Human Resource Management, Alexandria, VA. Used with permission. All rights reserved.

Design and composition by Greenleaf Book Group
Cover design by Greenleaf Book Group
Cover images: ©iStockphoto.com/AF-studio,
©iStockphoto.com/4x6, ©iStockphoto.com/Robert Churchill

Publisher's Cataloging Publication Data is available.

ISBN: 978-1-62634-205-7

Part of the Tree Neutral® program, which offsets the number of trees consumed in the production and printing of this book by taking proactive steps, such as planting trees in direct proportion to the number of trees used: www.treeneutral.com

TreeNeutral

Printed in the United States of America on acid-free paper

15 16 17 18 19 20   10 9 8 7 6 5 4 3 2 1

First Edition

Other Edition(s):
eBook ISBN: 978-1-62634-206-4

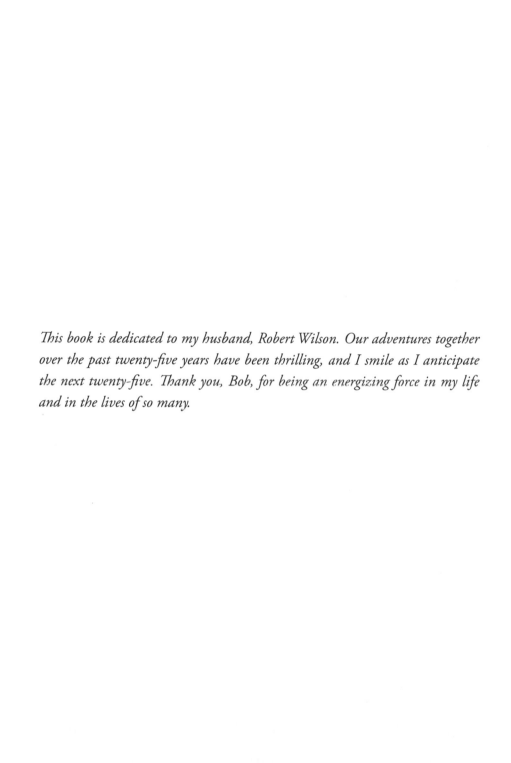

*This book is dedicated to my husband, Robert Wilson. Our adventures together over the past twenty-five years have been thrilling, and I smile as I anticipate the next twenty-five. Thank you, Bob, for being an energizing force in my life and in the lives of so many.*

# CONTENTS

# ACKNOWLEDGMENTS

Many wonderful people contributed to this book. I offer special thanks to the following:

Dr. Nicole Thompson, your research and interviewing prowess have brought *Energized Enterprise* to life. Your commitment to this project and your attention to detail were invaluable and much appreciated.

Thought leaders Vaughan Limbrick, Dr. Sharon Flinder, Dr. Garry Coleman, Dr. Altyn Clark, and Dr. William Bracken—you shared experiences and insights with me that inspired several passages and topics, and made the content more fun, interesting, and useful.

Janelle Millard, strategic initiatives director at TSI, you are indispensable in every aspect of our work, especially our publications. Without you leading the way on so many fronts, I could not have written this book while running a vibrant company.

Chris Benguhe, your wise counsel as my managing editor as I wrote the manuscript made the experience delightful and helped me take my work to the next level.

The Greenleaf Book Group team of Justin Branch, Neil Gonzalez, Emilie Lyons, Brandy Savarese, Carrie Jones, Steve Elizalde, and Corrin Foster: You are the best team ever!

I thank TSI's partners in community outreach and corporate social responsibility: American Red Cross, Easter Seals, Equal Footing Foundation, and March of Dimes. There are a million reasons why you are our charities of choice. The main reason is that you make a positive difference in our community every day.

Other leaders in the regional exchange of ideas to whom I express gratitude are the amazing stewards of the Northern Virginia Technology Council, Armed Forces Communications and Electronics Association, Inc. 5000, the National Defense Industrial Association, the Professional Services Council, the Small and Emerging Contractors Advisory Forum, the Society for Human Resource Management, the Marine Corps Association, the Virginia Chamber of Commerce, and the *Washington Business Journal*.

I'm particularly delighted to acknowledge the signature professionalism of TSI's talented employees, stellar teaming partners, committed service providers, and dedicated clients within the public-sector community. You inspire my work and the books that disseminate our collective knowledge.

Many thanks to every individual who reads this book. Here's to continued success on your leadership journey!

# PREFACE

Raised in a vibrant farming community, I loved working with my family to grow gorgeous heirloom flowers, fruits, and vegetables from an early age. That's when I started learning the value of the human element. Those experiences helped me realize that regardless of what is being produced, if people are clear about their mission and have shared values, the results of their labor can be amazing. As a young girl I was also curious about leadership, which drove me to read every historical biography in my grammar school library to learn everything I could about the lives of famous and important leaders.

Later, as I worked my way through school, I chose to specialize in leadership effectiveness for my doctorate in industrial-organizational psychology. Since completing my PhD in 1993, I have dedicated my career to being a leadership consultant while serving in many roles including CEO, board member, author, catalyst, coach, mentor, researcher, speaker, trainer, volunteer, and fundraiser. With insight into workplace psychology and the human element, I have lifted people to achieve their bold goals and helped leaders transform their organizations to boost enterprise performance and employee satisfaction.

Over the years, I've spoken and worked across the United States and around the world—from Scotland to Singapore and from South Africa to Canada—sharing my message and developing leaders. I've always felt in my heart that I wanted to devote my life to helping people maximize their potential and expand their talents. And when I assist leaders in maximizing and expanding their effectiveness, it truly fulfills my spirit. As their effectiveness increases, these leaders make a positive impact on the lives of the people in their workforces, and the state of the human condition improves every time that happens. That's why I became an industrial-organizational psychologist specializing in leadership effectiveness, and that's why I wake up every morning energized and ready to do the work that I've been called to do.

Elements of my message are also documented in my previous books, *Everybody's Business, Leaders in Motion,* and *The Transformation Desktop Guide.* Not only do I write leadership books, but I also run a company. Inspired by my passion for effective leadership, I launched Transformation Systems, Inc. (TSI). The TSI team has grown to be a successful company in the government market, made up of renowned engineers and psychologists with an extensive network of strategic partners. We have achieved multimillion-dollar annual revenues, at growth rates sometimes exceeding 60 percent. And I'm pleased to share that our growth continues as we expand our reach and impact by engaging more government executives in conversations about how to lead their organizations to greatness.

I love my company's mission to help leaders be their best, do great things, and have meaningful success. This mission energizes our team of PhDs and possibility thinkers to help government leaders achieve audacious goals in ways that are leaner, faster, better, and smarter. For five consecutive years, we've ranked in the top half of *Inc.* magazine's Fastest Growing Companies in America. We've also made the prestigious Virginia's Fantastic 50 list, and I have been honored by the *Washington Business Journal* as one of the twenty-five leading businesswomen in the DC metropolitan area. Also, we've been recognized repeatedly within the federal defense community for helping set historic records in counterterrorism efforts, for facilitating large-scale technology transitions, and much more.

With a passion for service, I get excited about helping our community thrive and making corporate social responsibility part of TSI's culture. With the aim of removing obstacles to leadership in our community, several years ago I launched TSI's FEED TO LEAD initiative, which nurtures leadership potential in those who need a helping hand. As part of this effort, the royalties from my books are donated to FEED TO LEAD's charities of choice. We're also a committed supporter of military veterans and their families through our community outreach work. As a result of our investment of time, talent, and treasure in FEED TO LEAD, we've been blessed with recognition including: Heroines of Washington Award (2011), National Jefferson Award for Public Service (2012), and the Fairfax County Chamber of Commerce Outstanding Corporate Citizenship Award (2013). These awards are much appreciated, but what's most important is the visibility they create for the great charities supported by FEED TO LEAD.

There you have it. I'm all about helping leaders be their best, do great things, and have meaningful success—including in the government sector. I decided to write this book because I believe government workplaces need to pay more attention to the human element—the workers themselves. And I believe it's not only possible, but critical. I'm certain that effective leadership will be the force to reenergize this dedicated and loyal workforce, because I know leaders are yearning to do this, and employees want and need it. I'm a true fan of government employees. They are tireless even when budgets are strained, funds are contracting, and changes are happening at an ever-faster rate. Furthermore, I know many leaders in government who wish to uplift their people as they identify affordable steps toward a happier enterprise. My objective is to help leaders thrive and exponentially magnify their impact as they lift their people to new heights. My ultimate dream is that leaders will bring their enterprises into balance with investments in human capital, yielding big returns in happiness, productivity, and innovation.

Now I've come full circle, back to the curious child who became the CEO and leadership author I am today. The perspective that I gained growing up in a vibrant farming community and studying successful leaders from the time I could read shaped how I see situations, solve problems, and design solutions. For instance, throughout government I see dedicated stewards of important agencies watching their people wilt and wither. These committed leaders know their "gardens" need care and feeding. Weeds of neglect are choking parts of the workforce because, due to budget cuts and downsizing, the human element hasn't been as consciously tended as it has been in other industries. But all workplaces can be transformed from barren to bountiful. There are ways to tend to the human element, cultivate the total system, and make the enterprise productively fruitful. Effective leadership is that solution, and it involves nurturing and growing the life force in government enterprises.

Effective leaders can transform even the most drab and lifeless deserts into colorful and productive fields of promise. And I'm convinced that our new government environment can become a colorful landscape of performance excellence. In the future, the human element can thrive in the government work environment as effective leaders sow the seeds of a new beginning in our nation's bureaucracies. Eventually, as our government's human capital gardens grow ever more abundant, our country can be a stronger leadership benchmark for all nations of the world. When I first shared the proposal for this book with people, they became very emotional, and I'm emotional about it too. I was touched by how impactful and relevant several influential leaders said it would be for the government workforce, and I trust that it will be meaningful and relevant for you and your enterprise. I believe this book will make a difference in your world, and I consider its message to be my personal visit to your workplace. I want to collaborate with you to improve your enterprise, and I'm confident that the information I'm sharing will allow that to happen.

Marta Wilson
Arlington, VA
February 2015

# HOW TO NAVIGATE THIS BOOK

You're busy—today you have fires to put out and dragons to slay. I want you to get the most from this book in the time you have. I understand you need to be productive in your quest to energize your enterprise. To help, I have divided this book into four parts.

**Part I, The Challenge**, outlines where we are today and pinpoints the issues that government leaders face. This section provides background information that can enhance your results.

**Part II, The Opportunity**, dives into fundamental principles of effective leadership and the human element.

If you have only one chance to sit down with this book, feel free to skip ahead to **Part III, The Solution**. This is where we are rolling up our sleeves and answering the "how."

**Part IV, The Future,** shows what is possible in an invigorated workforce and what happens when you create the magic. In addition, you will find questions for reflection, discussion, and action at the end of each chapter. My hope is that you approach this book as a tool chest and take what you need to fix the challenges you face.

# PART

## 1

# THE CHALLENGE

# GOVERNMENT EMPLOYEES DESERVE ATTENTION

## GET ME AN ASPIRIN!

Years ago, when I was a young consultant, I helped a member of the government's senior executive service, Mr. Jones, and two of his internal quality improvement change agents to design and develop a strategic planning and visionary retreat for his twenty-person leadership team. This was part of a long-term, large-scale, and enterprise-wide improvement effort. The first day of the off-site retreat, we worked on enhancing the organization's existing mission and vision statements.

Although, predictably, there were some raised voices and some drama on the first day, I was not fully prepared for what I saw on day two. One of the change agents, Harry (a GS-15 and the organization's director of total quality management), had been facilitating the leadership team to do a thorough first cut of a SIPOC analysis for the organization all morning. A SIPOC analysis portrays the organization's *suppliers*, *inputs*, *processes*, *outputs*, and *customers*, and it's a good tool to use in an improvement effort to help describe the current state of the total enterprise.

As the morning progressed, I could tell Mr. Jones was getting more and more frustrated with Harry and the analysis process. Mr. Jones was under a lot of stress due to deep budget cuts, problems with his staff, extreme pressure from his boss, and changes in government requirements that affected how his organization did business. His expressive eyebrows were hopping up and down. Finally, he tersely called a break and asked everyone to leave the room except for me and the other internal change agent, Randall (a young Lt. Commander). When the door closed, Mr. Jones screamed, "Please! Can one of you get me an aspirin?" We both jumped to attention and ran to the facilitator's tackle box that we always kept stocked with aspirin and many other tools and props critical for a successful management retreat. We watched Mr. Jones pop the aspirin, chase it with water, and put his head in his hands.

I asked, "How can we help you, sir?"

He was so angry. He yelled, "If Harry says SIPOC one more time, I am going to lose it! Do not let him back in front of the room! Do something, because this process is not working for me!" I'll admit I was rattled. After a quick chat with Randall, he and I decided that Harry would not be in front of the room for the remainder of the retreat, and we decided that completion of the SIPOC analysis would be put on hold. Although it needed to be done, we determined it could be completed later.

During that retreat and following it, I was torn about what was "right": what I thought was right, what Mr. Jones thought was right, and what Harry thought was right. Everybody, it seemed, wanted to move the enterprise forward, but the formal leader and one of the key change agents clearly valued different things, at least on the surface. After the retreat, I helped this organization improve in a meaningful way, achieve significant results, and make headway on many important fronts. This work included strategic planning, results measurement, process improvement, and also training and development of the people.

As far as the people front was concerned, in a leadership meeting following the offsite retreat, I realized I had to take a closer look at the human element and intervene to help lift the workforce to new heights. In this meeting, we were hearing from Berta, the team's ombudsman. Berta was sharing with Mr. Jones and the leadership team what she had learned from canvassing folks throughout the organization about the ongoing enterprise-wide change and improvement effort. Berta would say, "The people feel scared," and "The people are worried," and "The people are confused about the changes we're facing."

Suddenly, Mr. Jones, who as you know was under a lot of stress, pounded his fist on the table and yelled, "Berta! If you say 'the people' one more time, I . . ." We all froze. The silence was deafening. Berta took a deep breath, sat back in her chair, and did *not* look scared. Mr. Jones looked sheepish. He realized he was way out of line. I was excited to see Berta quietly and firmly stand both her ground and the people's ground. In the leadership team meetings to follow, Berta still represented the people and made sure their voices were heard throughout the multiyear change and improvement initiative. I became one of her biggest fans.

Mr. Jones, Berta, Harry, and Randall taught me a lot about formal and informal leadership. Through them and countless other clients over the past twenty years, I came to realize that improving the workplace requires clarity, commitment, and energy. It involves ongoing teamwork, appreciation for diversity, and the ability to manage stress. Over time my clients have helped me understand firsthand that the human element is the most important factor in every enterprise, no matter how large or how small. And that includes government agencies, where a focus on the human element is needed now more than ever.

## THE HUMAN ELEMENT REQUIRES CARE

The human element deserves attention and requires care, especially in the government workplace. In today's stressful environment, government employees' perceived quality of work life and their understanding of how they fit into the bigger picture are in danger of declining. As a result, there's a risk that productivity will take a turn for the worse. So if you walk through a government workplace and happen to see people who seldom smile, appear solemn, show a lack of energy, or even seem like they don't want to be there at all, you might ask yourself how and why it has come to this.

People in many pockets of the government workforce seem to feel helpless, and there appears to be a certain weight on them. It's predictable because this is a natural human response and psychological state precipitated by the daily stress and ambiguity that are endemic to bureaucratic institutions. Cause-and-effect relationships are hard to pinpoint, and quick fixes are not apparent. It's a complicated situation, and if these types of workplace problems were easily solved, someone would have already solved them. At the same time, most people who work in government seem as dedicated as ever to being public servants and as committed as ever to the missions of their organizations. Recent data collected by the United States Office of Personnel Management (OPM) supports this.

## RESULTS OF THE OPM FEDERAL VIEWPOINT EMPLOYEE SURVEY

In the spring of 2014, the OPM asked federal employees to provide their perspective on the business of government and to share their experience of what they see working and what needs to be fixed. Over 392,000 people responded to this Federal Employee Viewpoint Survey (FEVS).[1] While more than 60 percent of employees recommended their organization as a good place to work, stresses on public servants—including continued tight budgets and pay freezes—are reflected in the FEVS reports of global satisfaction.

Commenting on the results of the survey, Director of OPM Katherine Archuleta states, "This year, the two strongest results of the 2014 FEVS reveal that more than 90 percent of Federal employees are willing to put in the extra effort necessary to get the job done, and that they consistently look for ways to do better."[2] While the federal workforce still holds strong and positive views on many critical items, the combined voices of more than 392,000 employees cannot be dismissed.

The FEVS report from the previous year stated: "The survey results serve as an important warning about the long-term consequences of the sequestration and budget uncertainty. Without a more predictable and responsible budget situation, we risk losing our most talented employees, as well as hurting our ability to recruit top talent for the future."[3] This is a call to action, not only for federal leaders, but also for people like me who have expertise in the area of employee engagement and leadership effectiveness. In the chapters ahead, I'll share a path to help government leaders energize their enterprises.

## POCKETS OF HIGH AND LOW SATISFACTION

Is the federal government a model employer for the twenty-first century? It depends on where you look. There are pockets of high satisfaction and pockets of low satisfaction among government employees. Job satisfaction is critical for doing the public's business. Let's take a look at some extreme examples.

### Low Satisfaction at the Department of Homeland Security

The Department of Homeland Security (DHS) is an agency you might hope is staffed top to bottom by employees who like and have a passion for their jobs. Unfortunately, DHS employees have the lowest average morale in the federal government, according to the Government Accountability Office (GAO).[4]

In its report to Congress, the GAO cited data from the 2011 Federal Employee Viewpoint Survey indicating that "DHS employees had 4.5 percentage points lower job satisfaction and 7.0 percentage points lower engagement" in their work than other government workers. "Engagement," by the way, is "the extent to which employees are immersed in their work and spend extra effort on job performance."[5]

Especially unhappy and disengaged are employees of the Transportation Security Administration (TSA) and Immigration and Customs Enforcement (ICE). Perhaps most troubling, the survey showed that TSA's airport security screeners are 13 percentage points unhappier and 14 percentage points less engaged with their jobs than TSA's administrative office staff.

According to the GAO, since it began operations in 2003, the 200,000 employees of the DHS have consistently reported low job satisfaction. While acknowledging the DHS had made an effort to determine the root causes of its morale problems and had taken some corrective steps, the GAO suggested that the agency could beef up its analysis of metrics from the satisfaction survey results to achieve better action plans.

"We found that despite having broad performance metrics in place to track and assess DHS employee morale on an agency-wide level, DHS did not have specific metrics within the action plans that were consistently clear and measurable," stated the GAO in its report. "As a result . . . DHS's ability to assess its efforts to address employee morale problems and determine if changes should be made to ensure progress toward achieving its goals was limited."[6]

Specifically, the GAO recommended that when formulating plans to address morale, the DHS at least consider results from all of its various units, compare DHS results to similar organizations, and better address the root causes of low morale. According to the GAO, the DHS agrees with the recommendations.

## High Satisfaction at the National Aeronautics & Space Administration

Some of the most satisfied employees year-in, year-out work at NASA.[7] The 2014 FEVS report lists NASA as the highest-ranked employer for large agencies. According to John Palguta, vice president of policy with the Partnership for Public Service, which ranks hundreds of federal agencies each year in a report entitled *Best Places to Work*, "All the research shows that the more engaged employees are, the more committed they are, the more effective an organization is. The big driver in job satisfaction is leadership."[8]

This ranking, which reflects NASA's highest results since the FEVS report was developed, makes clear that the agency's workforce is focused on carrying out the nation's new and ambitious space program. "'The best workforce in the nation has made NASA the best place to work in federal government,' said NASA Deputy Administrator Lori Garver. 'Our employees are carrying out the nation's new strategic missions in space with heart-stopping landings on Mars, cutting-edge science and groundbreaking partnerships with American companies to resupplying the space station. They are truly leading in the innovation economy.'"[9]

## INSTANCES OF HIGH AND LOW PERFORMANCE

In addition to high and low satisfaction, there are instances of high and low performance within all government agencies. Outstanding work performance by employees leads to outstanding business results. Alternatively, poor work performance can contribute to an organization and its people winning a race to the bottom, and that's a race no one wants to win. Let's take a look at examples of performance from both ends of the continuum.

### Poor Performance at the Internal Revenue Service

An example of poor performance occurred at the Internal Revenue Service. In early May 2013, the Treasury Inspector General for Tax Administration released an audit report confirming that the IRS, in denying specific applications for tax exemption status, had used inappropriate criteria to identify potential political cases, including organizations with "Tea Party" in their names.[10] Media reports revealed that IRS officials in other regional offices had also been involved in targeting conservative groups and that a task force in Washington, DC, had overseen the activity.

After the Inspector General's audit report was made public, President Obama released a statement saying, "The IRS must apply the law in a fair and impartial way, and its employees must act with utmost integrity. This report shows that some of its employees failed that test."[11] The ethics and legality of what happened at the IRS notwithstanding, what we have here is a broken system in which people performed very poorly and in which leadership and management were not as effective as they could have been. These types of situations are opportunities for leaders and managers to lift people to new heights of performance.

## High Performance at the Department of Defense

At the other end of the performance continuum, let's look at an example of outstanding performance within the US Department of Defense (DoD) in which the Mine Resistant Ambush Protected (MRAP) Vehicle Program (JMVP) Joint Program Office (JPO MRAP) rapidly developed, acquired, and fielded the MRAP family of vehicles.

The JPO MRAP kept the requirements simple, clear, and flexible, plus they used mature technologies for great results and positive outcomes. In addition, everyone connected to the program had (and still has) a clear sense of the mission. In fact, in the early days of the program, it was common to see people working through the night and into the wee hours of the morning to keep everything moving and processes flowing. That's energizing!

## LEADERS CAN LIFT THEIR PEOPLE TO NEW HEIGHTS

Ideally, we would take a great performance and make it the standard. Wouldn't it be grand if all federal employees were as satisfied as the people at NASA, and wouldn't it be wonderful if every organization could have the mission success of the MRAP program? Our government's agencies allow employees to be engaged in extremely fulfilling missions such as maintaining a great national park system, wielding the world's best military, and exploring the frontier of space. These are missions that people can put their hearts into and dedicate their careers to accomplishing. We must bring effective leadership to everyone in government, including the high performers and the low performers alike.

Every workplace can be transformed from barren to bountiful. There is a proven solution for tending to the human element, cultivating the total system, and making the enterprise productively fruitful. Effective leadership is that solution, and it involves nurturing and growing the life force in federal enterprises. Science and industry abound with research and results showing how effective leadership can propel organizations to new heights during difficult times. Government executives can apply wisdom from science and industry to transform a workplace from a drab and lifeless desert (if that's their situation) into a colorful and productive field of promise.

The new government environment can become a colorful landscape of performance excellence as a result of effective leadership. Today, we have an opportunity for effective leaders to access and expand the untapped potential in their workforces to reach higher crests of individual, team, and enterprise performance. As a result, I envision a day when it's common for government executives to be sought out by science and industry as experts in leadership effectiveness.

In the future, the human element can thrive in the historically complex system of the federal work environment as effective leaders sow the seeds of a new beginning in our nation's bureaucracies. These trusted commanders of our government's enterprises will ensure that their people will blossom and flourish after adopting a discipline of effective leadership and putting it into practice. As our government's human capital gardens grow ever more abundant, our nation will become a benchmark for all, and the question, "Are *you* good enough for the government workforce?" will become the new mantra of people recruiting top talent from around the world.

## GET READY TO RELIEVE YOUR PAIN WITHOUT AN ASPIRIN

As you read what's ahead, you'll discover much more than an "aspirin" to remedy any headaches you may be experiencing due to the stresses and pressures of leadership. You'll learn about a holistic and scientific approach that's grounded in research and practice. This approach will not only stop your headaches before they start, but it will also help you lift your workforce to new heights of satisfaction and performance. Now, let's roll up our sleeves, dive in, and get to work on putting your plan for effective leadership into action.

## QUESTIONS FOR REFLECTION, DISCUSSION, AND ACTION

1. What are the biggest headaches for leaders in our organization?

2. What are the causes of the pain our leaders are experiencing?

3. How stressed are the people in our workforce, and how do we know?

4. How satisfied are the employees in our enterprise, and what are the signs?

5. What are some instances of high and low performance in our organization?

6. To what degree are we willing to invest in lifting our people's satisfaction and performance?

7. What are the possible outcomes of raising the satisfaction and performance of our workforce?

## 2

# BRIGHT STARS AND BLACK HOLES IN GOVERNMENT

## MISSION SUCCESS!

I love a good story, especially one with a hero who makes a difference. Here's a tale of innovation and excellence starring a gentleman named Ed. A few years back, Ed took a job as network operations leader at a large enterprise. This position was a big opportunity to create meaningful results using Ed's technical savvy and leadership skills. However, there were some obstacles that threatened his success. The team he was joining definitely lacked some understanding of the human element.

But Ed was a leader who built trust, shared his goals, and communicated how everyone fit into the tapestry of the organization. Once he built trust among his people, Ed knew that everybody could count on each other without constantly second-guessing motives and agendas. This allowed the workplace to be more efficient and effective.

Before arriving, Ed studied his roles and responsibilities. On day one, he began exploring everyone else's roles and the team structure. He quickly created his "First 100 Days in Office Goals." At the top of his list were meetings with everyone in his department, his peers, and his new boss to understand the organization. Although it can be good to make changes, Ed knew that a gangbuster approach could fail if he didn't understand the organization's existing politics, structure, and roles.

Ed's team dealt with high-level issues and managed all network connections. To understand their roles and responsibilities, Ed met with the fifty or so people who would be working for him, asking what was working, what wasn't, and why. He took pages of notes, and people saw that he wanted change. Ed knew that if people believed he wanted to make a difference, they would share information with him.

Assuring his staff that what they shared with him was confidential, Ed quickly gathered reams of information and realized that he had fifty people reporting to him with little to no effective management structure. So he established a clear reporting hierarchy, choosing five people to report to him directly. Ed identified the informal leaders, converted them into team leads, and helped them become official supervisors. People noticed these promotions and talked about positive changes that were taking place. As they saw Ed taking action and achieving results, their trust in him increased.

But there were still nagging holes in the human element of the organization. One individual gave up his new responsibilities as a team leader, realizing he didn't want to do what it took to lead. Ed then chose one of the youngest, newest, and most energetic team members. Everyone was shocked when he gave her full authority to do what was needed to achieve mission success. Today, that individual is one of the department's biggest success stories.

Before his arrival, Ed's team had gained a reputation for poor client service. When people would ask for help, Ed's team would demand certain things from them before working on the issues. So Ed enrolled the team to adopt a discipline around critical processes such as a daily supervisor checklist, client service initiatives, enforcing current rules, inspecting what's expected, updating voice mail daily, carrying phones at all times, plus updating vision and mission statements. As a result, the team became more responsive and customer focused.

Another challenge was that Ed's division, operations, had a poor relationship with the planning division. Ed discovered this in the staff interviews, and in response he established weekly meetings with planning. In these meetings, Ed and the attendees took actions to increase the effectiveness of their working relationship. This resulted in a healthy relationship, and these meetings became a standard in the organization.

Additionally, as he met with everyone, one issue Ed uncovered was a tendency for people to procrastinate. For example, once a project was completed in planning, it could take six months to get a technology turned over to Ed's group. From a client service perspective, that was unacceptable.

To solve this, Ed assigned every one of his engineers a project. He said, "If the project is not immediately turned over to us when it's time for acceptance from planning, I will hold you personally accountable. This will require you to work closely with planning to communicate our standards." Beginning with the day he implemented accountability, every project that came in was accepted immediately. The change was like flipping a switch, and this huge problem disappeared, resulting in more success for Ed's team.

Ed continued removing obstacles, making sure his team could get work done, and putting processes in place so they could be more effective and efficient. He required detailed documentation of work flow and policies, which allowed folks to make most decisions without seeking approval. As more guidelines were put in place, it freed up time to spend on strategic issues versus tactical issues. On day one, tactical issues took about 90 percent of Ed's time. Three years later, this had been reduced to 30 percent, which was great.

Finally, Ed focused on training, which builds morale and competence. With training, people know they will have opportunities for additional responsibility and the potential to make more money. They benefit by growing technically. They feel good about *not* having to learn everything on their own time or pay for it with their own resources. As a result, everyone is more competent, has higher morale, and is more competitive for promotions. When Ed first came in, his department did not have a well-defined training plan. So he created a training outline and conducted a training needs assessment. Then he turned it over to one of his reports to lead an outstanding in-house training program.

From year one to year three, there was continuous improvement in Ed's group. They updated old processes, strengthened relationships, and drove organizational change. Ed clearly expressed what he expected from client-service, training, vendor-relations, and budgetary perspectives. He built trust, enrolled people, set goals, documented processes, and defined roles. He also established accountability, communicated effectively, measured performance, and championed training. Empowered people became the life force of the workplace, and Ed saw his team's effectiveness escalate as they reached peak performance and mission success.

However, Ed warns, it is important to adopt a discipline that empowers and aligns people because it promotes self-awareness, builds community, and inspires dedication. This is because with little or no alignment of critical systems, empowerment and change can result in confusion and disorder. We see this in government today. Lack of systems alignment and other factors contribute to the trials, tribulations, and headaches experienced by leaders in government at all levels. Let's explore some of these challenges.

## BLACK HOLES THAT THREATEN GOVERNMENT'S BRIGHT STARS

It's important for us to look at some factors that, if not addressed, threaten to extinguish many of the bright stars in government. Ed is one of those bright stars who encountered a lot of difficulties that exist in federal government, and we need to address those factors. I think of these factors as black holes because black holes prevent anything, including light, from escaping.

Within government, there are four realities, or black holes, that have the potential to dampen the brilliance of bright stars such as Ed. The first reality is that complex systems are very difficult to lead and manage. Second, poor performance is extremely challenging to address across all agencies. Third, many people are stretched way too thin as a result of budget cuts and staff reductions. And fourth, new technologies are slow to be adopted and implemented. Let's take a closer look at these four threats.

## Complex Systems Are Difficult to Lead and Manage

Both big and cumbersome, the very nature of government has made it unwieldy and difficult to lead and to manage. In such a complex system, ongoing redundancy, waste, and abuse are difficult to discover, measure, and monitor. Also, in many cases, large acquisitions and critical programs are extremely difficult to execute. For example, "complex defense and network-centric systems," such as the Army's Future Combat System, the Coast Guard's Integrated Deepwater System, and the Federal Aviation Administration's Next Generation Air Traffic System, were extremely ambitious and riddled with challenges.

"Such systems are difficult to develop and oversee. They incorporate technology that was not created when the systems were" in development. These programs are brought to life "by a team of government managers and industry practitioners, aided by" engineers and scientists, "overseen by" politicians, "monitored by auditors, and evaluated in life-and-death situations." This work is not for the faint of heart.

"For the government," managers "struggle to keep up as complexity blossoms, often resulting in blown budgets and missed schedules." This is due to the "difficulty of creating systems comprised of thousands of elements, addressing dozens or hundreds of requirements, produced by multiple manufacturers."[1] Often, this complexity contributes to poor performance.

## Poor Performance Is Challenging to Address

Regarding less-than-top talent, ask anyone in government, and they'll tell you that terminating an employee for poor performance has never been easy. The laborious process of removing unproductive individuals, even with documentation of inferior work, has made it practically impossible to remove poor performers from the federal workplace.

Years ago, there were good reasons behind this. "Federal officials at the time of the Gilded Age created the civil service as a way to insulate government workers from the influence of politics. The Pendleton Act and the Civil Service Act of 1883 established the merit-based system, which ended the practice of awarding government jobs as political favors and led to the system that is currently in place."[2]

Managers have little incentive to go through the time-consuming process of firing people. Statistically, firing federal workers is rare. In 2012, just 0.4 percent of civilian employees were fired. "Federal employees' job security is so great that workers in many agencies are more likely to die of natural causes than get laid off or fired," reported *USA Today* after a 2011 study of federal employment statistics.[3]

According to Chris Edwards of the Cato Institute: "There are fundamental incentive problems for why the firing rate is so low . . . The taxpayers are paying for federal workers' salaries, but there aren't incentives to fire people—it's unpleasant firing people, but here in the private sector there's pressure for you to do it because you're losing money if you don't."[4] This reality has often resulted in having the wrong people on the bus in government agencies. And if the wrong people are on the bus, it makes getting to the desired destination a lot more difficult and unpleasant.

## Many People Are Stretched Way Too Thin

In addition, for years now, many agencies government-wide have been asked to do more with less, and as a consequence, lots of people have become overworked. In many cases, employees wear more than one hat. In doing so, they attempt to keep multiple domains of responsibility from spinning out of control while they stretch to keep everything glued together and operating as smoothly as possible.

For example, a recent report found that federal performance improvement officers (PIOs) "spend less than half their time on performance manage-ment because many have other responsibilities within their agencies. . . . [Survey] respondents said mandates to report to Congress are a hindrance because the information often is not used constructively." Instead, agencies need reliable performance measurement systems that produce meaningful results.[5]

This is just one example of willing workers being stretched to the max, which keeps them from making the biggest positive impact possible. When people are stretched too thin, it impacts the speed at which change can occur and at which new technologies can be adopted.

## New Technologies Are Slow to Be Adopted

Government agencies tend to be slow in adopting technologies, as illustrated in a recent study that explored adoption of new and innovative technolo-gies among federal government decision makers. This research, conducted by Market Connections, revealed the perception of technology adoption in government agencies as "slow and difficult to keep going." According to *Information Week*, the public sector still trails the private sector in its adop-tion of cloud computing. A study conducted by Redshift Research found "only 23 percent of the public sector is using cloud computing, versus 42 percent of the private sector companies."[6]

Issues such as "fear of the unknown, lack of operational control over data and applications, and worry about the reliability of the technology" are bar-riers to adoption of cloud computing. The government sector also "lacks the cloud-computing expertise that is more available in the private sector, which could account for slower adoption and less satisfaction among those respondents."[7]

Clearly, there is much work to be done to ensure our government is able to quickly facilitate technology transitions smoothly and quickly. As we keep these black holes that threaten bright stars in the back of our minds, let's examine a few more examples of great performance in government.

## BRIGHT STARS SHINE ACROSS ALL AGENCIES

Across government, there are many success stories of excellence in finance, procurement, human capital management, quality, and leadership. These stories star heroes who build trust, enroll people, set goals, and establish accountability. They communicate effectively, inspect what's expected, and ensure education is a priority. Some great examples include the stories of recipients of Service to America medals.[8] Awarded annually by the Partnership for Public Service to honor the accomplishments and commitment of America's outstanding public servants, these medals send a powerful message about the importance of a strong civil service and inspire a new generation of Americans to serve. Three outstanding medal recipients are Louis Milione, Elliott Branch, and Charles Scoville. Here are their stories and some of the lessons learned.

### Louis Milione

Louis Milione is a special agent and group supervisor for the Drug Enforcement Administration. He received the 2012 Samuel J. Heyman Service to America for Justice and Law Enforcement Medal. Mr. Milione "led a high-stakes federal undercover investigation spanning three continents resulting in the arrest and conviction" of Viktor Bout, known as "the world's most notorious arms trafficker."

"Bout was considered untouchable. United States and international authorities for years sought to capture . . . Bout, a notorious arms trafficker and former Soviet military officer. He was known as the 'Merchant of Death' for selling weapons to the Taliban, Libyan dictator Muammar Gaddafi, Hezbollah, and to vicious despots, warlords, and human rights abusers. In 2007, U.S. national security officials turned to the Drug Enforcement Administration (DEA), which had been gathering information on Bout and launched an investigation.

"At the center of this high-stakes undercover sting was Louis Milione. He coordinated activities with law enforcement and government officials in the U.S. and abroad, and provided assistance during the lengthy extradition proceedings and criminal prosecution. 'Lou Milione is one of the most tenacious and skilled supervisors at the DEA. It was his leadership that brought down this horrific arms trafficker,' said DEA Administrator Michele Leonhart."[9]

Louis Milione's leadership resulted in outstanding results, and he and his team could proudly declare mission success. Although not everyone wants or could do Milione's job, everyone can benefit from this book's best practices on how leaders like him conceive a plan, manage multiple stakeholders, leverage technology, and manage ambiguity.

Now, another bright star.

## Elliott Branch

Elliott Branch is deputy assistant secretary of acquisition and procurement for the US Navy, and I met with him recently to discuss leadership effectiveness. Mr. Branch received the 2012 Samuel J. Heyman Service to America Management Excellence Medal from the Partnership for Public Service. To ensure mission success for the Navy, he "leads savvy acquisition and procurement that ensure our warfighters have the right equipment when they need it, at the best possible value for the American taxpayer.

"Our warfighters need the right equipment to fulfill their missions and return home safely. Branch ensures they are properly equipped at the best possible value as he stands watch over this huge and complex undertaking. He helps shape every major acquisition, negotiates with the major defense contractors and makes sure the Navy and Marines are getting what they need in a timely fashion and at the best possible price.

"'Everything the Navy buys goes through his shop. He ensures goals are met across-the-board and within budget,' said Sean Stackley, the assistant secretary of the Navy for research, development and acquisition. 'He's always looking to drive down the cost of doing business and to get a better deal for the department.'

"Over the years, Branch has been credited with a number of highly successful negotiations and important management innovations. He led negotiations to consolidate production of a class of guided missile destroyers to a single shipyard. According to Stackley, the consolidation resulted in $1.5 billion in savings and ensured stability in the industry as other shipyards transitioned to new contracts."[10]

Mr. Branch's many contributions and accomplishments over time have contributed to the DoD's mission success. Mr. Branch's domain of responsibility is vast, yet leaders at all levels can benefit from how best to shape major initiatives, negotiate with all stakeholders, and make sure customers are getting what they need quickly and at the best price.

Now, on to our final star.

## Charles Scoville

Another hero is Charles Scoville, who is chief of amputee patient care service at Walter Reed National Military Medical Center, and who I recently observed in action when I toured Walter Reed with leaders of the American Red Cross. Dr. Scoville received the medal for National Security and International Affairs. His work "enables combat amputees to lead active lives and potentially return to duty, through an internationally recognized rehabilitation program that uses a novel sports medicine approach.

"Combat amputees have come back from Iraq and Afghanistan physically and emotionally devastated. Dr. Scoville has helped them find new hope and reach new heights. The building . . . where young athletes are engaged in intensive training activities is not an Olympic workout facility, but an advanced center for military amputees—part of a unique rehabilitation program for amputees that he designed and developed.

"Dr. Scoville oversees the staff that works with about 170 amputees and has helped drive the research into advances in prostheses. Some of the 1,450 injured service members who have been through the program have gone on to complete triathlons, climb Mt. Everest and compete in gymnastics, skiing, rowing and other sports. More than 300 have gone back into military service, and 53 have redeployed into Iraq or Afghanistan, including one individual with an above-the-knee amputation who went on to lead 350 Marines overseas.

"'He gives folks new hope that they can function and strive for independence,' said Brigadier General Joseph Caravalho."[11] A true hero, this leader is lifting our nation's wounded warriors to new heights of recovery and succeeding in his mission to make a meaningful difference in the lives of veterans and their families.

Even though Dr. Scoville's amazing work is beyond the scope of many people's jobs, there are proven practices used by him and other exceptional leaders that all people can apply to their enterprises to enroll, build, grow, and train diverse teams that create mission success.

### People Are Making a Meaningful Difference

We see individuals like the winners of these Service to America awards every day in government. There are many examples of heroic and effective leaders, and we can't forget that there are countless public servants making a difference. The role models of great performance across all agencies are to be celebrated and emulated. At the same time, the factors that threaten great workforce performance must be addressed. Leadership will be the key to solving this puzzle.

## LEADERS HAVE A FRUSTRATING PUZZLE TO SOLVE

There are bright stars that exemplify great performance, and there are black holes that threaten to engulf those stars and weaken the federal system, making it vulnerable to a plethora of performance issues. In some agencies, the situation is worse than in others. However, one thing is true across the board. No stakeholders—including citizens, elected politicians, government employees, or their leaders—wish for a federal workforce that is unhappy and unproductive. Everybody would embrace a new beginning in which workforce potential is unleashed as in the heroic vignettes I've shared with you. This new beginning would strengthen the total system without blindly mimicking the private sector, which has its own pros, cons, strengths, and weaknesses.

Currently, in the federal sector, many forward-thinking executives are watching less-than-motivated talent rotate in and out of their organizations, and they're seeing that employee disengagement can cost billions annually in productivity losses. Dedicated stewards of our government's enterprises are watching many of their people wander, wilt, and wither. And they want to know what to do about it without changing the total system's core structure. They want to know how to create results like Louis Milione, Elliott Branch, and Charles Scoville.

This is a puzzle to solve, and it has many pieces. Yes, there are pockets of high performance across government. However, the federal landscape is bleak, budgets are strained, and the marketplace is filled with apprehension. As fiscal forces threaten the government's ability to address human capital issues, stewardship of this vast workforce is at risk. Resources are limited, funds are contracting, and changes are happening at an ever-faster rate. Now more than ever, leaders need the knowledge and tools in the chapters ahead to ensure sustained mission success and allow the bright stars to multiply and spread throughout the federal government.

## QUESTIONS FOR REFLECTION, DISCUSSION, AND ACTION

1. What are the threats to the bright stars in our organization?

2. What are some examples of employees who are shining brightly?

3. What are we doing to address threats to our people's satisfaction and performance?

4. What are we doing to reward and recognize stellar performance?

5. What else could we do to remove threats to employee performance?

6. How could our stellar performers help lift others to perform at higher levels?

7. How could our leaders, managers, and supervisors enable more stellar performers to emerge throughout the enterprise?

# TURBULENT WATERS
# THREATEN EVERY ENTERPRISE

## PLEASE HURRY!

Before I started writing this book, I reached out to a few trusted government executives. In addition to sharing a summary of the book's concept, I also asked them what they're experiencing during these turbulent times and if they believe my expertise can help federal leaders. Here is a note I received from one of those individuals:

Dear Dr. Wilson,

In the privacy of my office at the Pentagon, I quietly consumed this summary. For reasons I still do not understand, the "Energized Enterprise" journey you outline resonates with me at a deeply personal and emotional level. My excitement and interest in this topic may not resonate with as many people on the planet as it should because too many people have never experienced the incredible joy and magnificence of accomplishments on a massive scale. The breadth and depth of cultural cynicism and poor leadership is bountiful. The world needs this book.

I have come to believe that the most effective endeavors in public service occur when leadership enables and promotes individual fulfillment simultaneously with organization goals— value alignment precedes attitudes, precedes behaviors, and grows culture. The most effective experiences and undeniable success require leaders to weave humanity into their work. Relationships, nurturing, and methods that cause individuals to grow while simultaneously fulfilling public service is massively exciting and truthfully should be of great interest to the entire executive force.

All the descriptors that characterize the potential for experiencing humanity and loveliness—passion, compassion, fulfillment, inspiration—are especially exciting to me. There are enablers to professional and personal self-esteem that are absolutely nourished or crushed in the workplace. My excitement for this book is especially profound because I actually believe I will be a more capable, happier, fulfilled practitioner of this very difficult vocation while causing profound outcomes that make the world a better place.

The only phrases that I imagined revolve around "cultural excellence" and perpetuating an experience in the workplace that grows with the world and enables programs of attraction. The "Energized Enterprise" will be a wonderful therapeutic tool to help the nation . . . and, even more importantly, the people who make it great . . . have an incredible experience that will make their lives worthwhile. In two words . . . my gut . . . with real tears . . . "totally awesome." Please hurry!

Very humbly,
George

## PERFORMANCE IS AT RISK

Not only did George's note touch my heart, but it also convinced me that, now more than ever, I want to exponentially magnify the bright stars in the public sector. My mission is to help them successfully traverse the rising waters of uncertainty they face each day. This note from my friend and colleague validates for me personally that executives face big challenges and that performance is at risk in federal agencies. During our government's economic crisis, widespread sadness, general anxiety, and waning productivity permeate the workforce.

In fact, the dominant finding by government-focused researchers is that public-sector productivity has not kept pace with that of the private sector.[1] "A recent survey by McKinsey & Company in partnership with *Government Executive* magazine discovered that federal employees are highly motivated but accountability is lacking."[2] In agencies where employees are motivated but lack accountability, productivity still suffers.

In addition to accountability and productivity issues, the workforce is being reduced. Also, leaders are struggling to help people innovate, manage low performers, and keep high performers motivated. Leaders are watching their organizations lose contractor support and government staff due to reduced funding, required downsizing, and even job-hopping. These challenges are serious and require effective leadership.

## WORKERS ARE ANXIOUS

While struggling to lead improvement in a terrain laden with fiscal cliff landmines, government executives seek to relieve the anxiety being felt in the workplace. With pots of money that have previously funded human capital stewardship shrinking or vanishing, it's tough to lead important initiatives or to hire the contractor support needed to ensure successful implementation of those initiatives. It's hard to move forward or drive change in this environment.

When contractors struggle in this way, it adversely impacts the effectiveness of government and its employees.[3] Support contractors make up a large percentage of the government workforce, and they are anxious. Contracts are being scrutinized more heavily and renewed at lower levels. In fact, Deltek's 2013 GovCon Industry Study found that companies working in the federal space continue to navigate through an ever-shifting maze of scope changes, work schedule adjustments, and other contract modifications.

Government employees are anxious too. At least two dozen federal agencies, including the Department of Labor, Environmental Protection Agency, Federal Aviation Administration, Federal Bureau of Investigation, and Department of Defense issued furlough notices in 2013.[4] This is part of a larger effort to trim $1.2 trillion from federal deficits over ten years. This impacts the lives of many employees, who will have to give up flexible work schedules during the furlough period and take a pay cut. On the one hand, many people still have jobs. On the other hand, this reality does not promote motivation or satisfaction. Instead, it promotes fear and uncertainty.

## INNOVATION IS DIFFICULT

In many cases, government executives don't have the support they need for innovative solutions or 100 percent mission accomplishment. The increased use of lowest price contracts means the quality of contractor support is becoming significantly lower. Many federal leaders find they can't count on the level of performance they've had in the past.

Contractors aren't the only ones struggling with how to provide innovative solutions. It's a challenge for government employees as well. *Federal Computer Week* recently stated, "Are some federal managers so risk-averse that they can't tolerate creativity even if the alternative is mediocrity? Or do they lack the means by which to offer beyond-the-norm rewards for beyond-the-norm thinking? It's probably fair to say that as far as employees are concerned, there is no right answer."[5]

So federal executives are faced with leading both contractors and employees who want to bring innovation to the table in a system that doesn't necessarily promote it. This puts leaders in a position where it's challenging to be effective. In the government system, it's hard for leaders to cocreate a collective, innovative sense of mission and vision. It's difficult for them to encourage people to achieve more than what's thought possible. It isn't easy to inspire folks to approach matters in innovative ways.

However, these are the behavioral standards to which effective leaders hold themselves. Effective leaders are committed to inspiring, encouraging, and collaborating to help their people make their best contributions. For many leaders with outstanding potential, it's a conundrum, and they are at a loss about how to unleash their potential and others' potential to achieve collective, meaningful success in operating their agencies at peak performance.

## THERE ARE PROBLEMS WITH HIGH AND LOW PERFORMERS

### High Performers

During economic downturns, it can be hard for stellar employees to be motivated. With a reduced workforce, meeting acceptable levels of productivity can be difficult for superstar employees, especially when they're asked to do more with less. In turn, it can be very difficult for leaders to stay focused and do the things that help people be their best and do great things.

It's hard to communicate effectively during unsettled times, and yet the most effective and productive employees expect open, honest, and direct communication, or else their motivation is affected. It's also difficult to pay attention to top performers' unique contributions, and leaders are looking for best practices they can put in motion to help value-adding employees understand how their individual efforts contribute to the direction of the enterprise. It requires effort and dedication to involve everybody during uncertain times when budgets are tight, but superstars need to feel included. Finally, during stressful times, high-performing employees want to know that everything is in control, that leaders have looked at the right information, and that they have used it to make the best decisions for the enterprise. Otherwise, their motivation suffers.

## Low Performers

Because it can be so difficult to terminate government employees who are poor performers, leaders are often faced with the decision to either promote these folks or send them to training. This rewards poor individual performance and negatively affects organizational results. It's draining. It also flies in the face of everything we know about perceptions of equity, procedural fairness, and workplace motivation.

Budget cutbacks haven't helped this situation and possibly add to the challenge that leaders face when dealing with substandard work. Faced with the distractions of funding cuts, it's tough for leaders to focus in on what's best for poor performers. It's also hard to spend the time needed to raise poor performers to higher levels of productivity. And it's difficult to act as a mentor, providing the caring, compassion, and empathy that positively influence people's job performance.

However, now is the time to get serious about employees with chronic performance issues.[6] As hard as it may seem, given the distractions of reduced budgets, increased demands, and sequestration, poor performance does require attention. In the chapters that lie ahead, we'll talk about how to stay focused and be prepared to do what it takes to address employees whose work is below standard.

This includes the best way to tell someone that his or her performance or behavior is unacceptable. You'll also learn about best practices to establish clear expectations and accountability with people. In addition, we'll cover how to best document all performance issues and to inspect what's expected. This is knowledge that leaders must have, and paying proper attention to poor performers doesn't go unnoticed by high-performing superstars. In fact, the bright stars take note of and are motivated by fair treatment toward everyone in the organization.

## MISSIONS ARE FAILING

In addition to issues with high- and low-performing individuals, the problems in government are widespread and systemic. The proof is in the systemic failures that are showing up. For example, the Federal Protective Service (FPS) collects over $200 million annually "from agencies to perform security threat assessments on federal buildings, but the agency is failing to perform that job, according to a new audit report.

"'FPS currently is not assessing risk at the over 9,000 federal facilities under the custody and control of [the General Services Administration (GSA)] in a manner consistent with federal standards,' says the Government Accountability Office [(GAO)] . . . GAO recommends that FPS incorporate a wide range of security factors into any permanent security assessment tool it develops, develop a new comprehensive system for contract guard oversight, and coordinate with GSA and other agencies to reduce duplicative security assessments."[7]

Thinking back to Ed's story and what he did during his first one hundred days on the job, the FPS is an example of fertile ground for an approach that involves updating old processes, strengthening relationships, and driving organizational change. FPS might also benefit from inspecting what's expected from client-service, training, vendor-relations, and budgetary perspectives. Finally, establishing more accountability and communicating more effectively could only help this situation.

## COMPLAINTS ARE RISING

An inevitable outcome when systems fail is that employees will be dissatisfied. "A report from the Congress's Office of Compliance shows that hostile work environment complaints are rapidly increasing. In 2010, 168 federal employees filed a complaint against their employers, and in 2011 that number jumped to 196 employees . . . One employee, a disabled veteran, hired through the Wounded Warrior Project, wrote a resignation letter that said she would 'rather be at war in Afghanistan' than stay in the office and deal with the hostile work environment created by her boss."[8]

Government agencies can be very stressful work environments where employees hold many responsibilities. They have a lot to account for, and the high-anxiety workplace can result in contentious relationships between employees and their superiors. However, adapting to differences among people and creating a healthy workplace boils down to treating people with respect.

Respect is the cornerstone of the best work environments. Treating people with respect sometimes means treating them as we would like to be treated. More often, it means treating them as *they* would like to be treated. Ideally, there's a midpoint where everyone feels respected. This requires that leaders ask questions, listen, and consciously refine behaviors, which we'll discuss more in the chapters to follow.

## SERVICES ARE SHRINKING

The only thing that could make a failing system worse is fewer resources, and that's what's happening. As reported by CNS News and the Associated Press, automatic spending cuts that took effect in the spring of 2013 are expected to touch a vast range of government services. For example, "hundreds of illegal immigrants have been freed from jail across the country. Immigration and Customs Enforcement officials say they had reviewed several hundred cases of immigrants and decided to put them on an 'appropriate, more cost-effective form of supervised release.' . . . There could be an estimated 2,100 fewer food safety inspections and increased risks to consumers because of the cuts. The nation's busiest airports could be forced to close some of their runways, causing widespread flight delays and cancellations. Visiting hours at all 398 national parks could be cut and sensitive areas blocked off to the public.

"More than half of the nation's 2.1 million government workers may be required to take furloughs as agencies trim budgets. Millions of taxpayers may not be able get responses from Internal Revenue Service call centers and taxpayer assistance centers. Veterans' funerals at Arlington National Cemetery could be cut to 24 a day from 31, meaning delays in burials for troops from past wars."[9]

This is not a pretty picture. However, no matter how difficult the times, leaders must rely on honesty to keep things glued together. This requires leaders to communicate what they think and feel to their people. People will trust what is said, even if they don't like it.

Offering honest thoughts, feelings, and ideas ensures that employees are getting the true facts. When they know the facts, people are resilient and creative in helping solve problems. Later on, we'll discuss the power of open, honest, and direct communication in helping everyone see what's possible during times of difficulty and crisis. For some leaders, this will require getting out of their comfort zones.

## LEADERS ARE IN A QUANDARY ABOUT WHAT TO DO

Turbulent waters of uncertainty threaten our government's workforce, where the human element has needed attention for some time. Now the problem is exacerbated by federal budget cuts. Decision makers want and need to know how to rescue and revive their people within the confines of a complex system during an economic crisis. With everything that's happening, many government executives realize they can't afford to go another day without protecting and nourishing the human potential within their enterprises.

Agencies are at risk of losing intellectual capital, and because of this, leaders need retention strategies that work. Today's workforce is motivated by different factors than past generations, and government organizations need to match benefits and work-life balance with what people need, expect, and demand in line with current best practices. Government workers must be engaged and accountable to improve performance, and leaders need to understand the best ways to enroll and align everyone in the organization. During the economy's downturn and its subsequent recovery, government leaders must continue to drive change, and they need to know which tools and methods are best for creating sustainable improvement.

Effective leaders must invest time, caring, compassion, and empathy to properly address myriad issues. Many admirable leaders are in a quandary. On the one hand, they know there's a better way. On the other hand, they are distracted from implementing what they know is right as they fight operational fires and struggle to keep things glued together in the face of funding cuts across their agencies. How do leaders move forward?

## COMFORT ZONES CAN HOLD LEADERS BACK

The status quo isn't going to work. That can be a very tough thing to accept, especially for good leaders. But the situation in some organizations is extreme. Good leaders must step up and adapt. They must be prepared to let go of comfort, choosing effectiveness over the status quo. When faced with the chance to step outside their comfort zones, leaders must exert their will over their habits. That's how leaders choose consciously to react in new ways. Each time leaders confront this choice, they must decide all over again whether or not to lead. And they must act.

Pushing to be one's best during turbulent times is a crucial commitment for leaders, and it involves continuous change. Change is uncomfortable, even for leaders. Sometimes, in fact, change is even more painful for leaders. Every day offers new challenges to effectiveness that require leaders to choose whether to improve or to entrench. Every new improvement opportunity invites leaders to venture into unknown territory and get outside their comfort zones.

A comfort zone is a belief that develops as people learn to relate to the world around them. A comfort zone can be crucial. Touching a hot stove with a bare hand, a child quickly learns to believe that doing so in the future will result in another painful burn. This particular comfort zone (hot stoves are dangerous) protects children from injury. However, comfort zones can hold leaders back. As evolution tugs leaders into the unknown, their comfort zones tempt them to reach for what they know. If they choose comfort over growth, they may be opting for the greater risk.

For leaders, most comfort zones do not remain as constant as the danger of a hot stove. Circumstances change, and what is comfortable—and safe— changes too. Comfort zones often are constructed from past circumstances. In an effort to cling to safety, leaders often don't realize they are becoming less safe by not changing. Thus comfort zones, if left unquestioned, can limit leaders and can even harm them and their organizations.

Leaders must try new methods that take them beyond comfort. This requires experimentation. Challenging oneself to experiment with new strategies is the best way to inspire others, and inspiration is what government employees need, now more than ever. Leaders must access, expand, unite, and guide their potential to achieve mission success. However, leaders have many questions, and they need answers.

## GREAT HUMAN CAPITAL STRATEGIES CAN HELP

It all comes down to the human element, and attending to the human element requires a strategy. A good human capital strategy blends appraisal, research, and analysis to assess the organization's current workforce circumstances. It produces solutions that focus on workforce alignment, while implementing plans to support succession, onboarding, and career and talent development.

Measurable effects of attending to the human element include staff satisfaction, engagement, and retention. Approaches include individual coaching, executive workshops, training seminars, and advancement plans. People can enjoy and benefit from this kind of development. There are fundamentals at work in human capital strategies, and tried and true options exist for government.

If leaders want results, they need the best talent management skills possible. No matter how much leaders acknowledge the human element or how they choose to incorporate the process into their enterprises, human capital strategy is doomed to be just one more plan, indeed just one more empty ritual, unless it plays out in a vibrant cultural dialogue that motivates, inspires, and magnifies greatness in all of the organization's people.

Human capital risks include lack of knowledge and leadership depth across the organization. Protracted and unclear development paths for staff are another risk. Poor alignment of talent to priorities and strategy is another. The greatest risk is when people aren't talking to each other about what is possible.

In the best scenario, government leaders solve the puzzle. In the worst scenario, the current talent mix proves unable to support the long-term objectives of government organizations. Collaboration is the way to ensure that dialogue in any agency isn't idle chatter or bitter grievance. Leaders must get outside their comfort zones and drive conversations and behaviors that magnify individual, team, and enterprise performance. Effective leaders achieve stability and minimize risk by developing current talent, ensuring succession during attrition, and retaining their best talent. This is true in periods of transition and growth. It is also true in periods of economic strain.

My assertion to leaders who want to change the current state is "Hurry!" There is no time to waste. Now is the time to put into practice the tools, tips, and techniques in this book. You can create great strategies that lift the human element in your organization to shine its brightest. Get ready to challenge your comfort zone and experiment with new behaviors that drive mission success. Fasten your seat belt, and prepare for liftoff!

## QUESTIONS FOR REFLECTION, DISCUSSION, AND ACTION

1. How are we supporting our high performers? How's that working for us?

2. How are we supporting our low performers? How's that working for us?

3. How would we rate ourselves on achieving total mission success? Is there a gap, and if so, how would we describe it?

4. What complaints are we receiving from our employees, and how are we addressing them?

5. Are our services shrinking due to budget constraints, and if so, how is it affecting our organization's effectiveness?

6. Are we open to experimenting with new ways to help our people and our organization be more effective? If so, what risks are we willing to take?

7. What are the key elements of our human capital strategy? Is our strategy driving results, and how do we know?

# PART

## 2

# THE OPPORTUNITY

# THE BEDROCK OF LEADERSHIP
# IS THE HUMAN ELEMENT

## EUREKA!

Effective leaders understand human nature, and they create connections even in difficult situations. For example, when promoted to lead a new organization, one of our colleagues, Ellen, inherited an adversarial culture. In this new job, she led and managed brilliant scientists who were working on different research projects, and each research group was very competitive with all the other groups. On top of this, Ellen was the first minority female promoted into her position, and she knew there were plenty of qualified people who felt entitled to the promotion that she had earned.

Given the situation, Ellen wanted to set things up for success from the beginning. She decided to tackle it by providing leadership training for all her employees as part of a larger annual gathering. In that training, small working groups were each asked to solve a problem that Ellen, their new boss, faced, and to look at it from her point of view. Most of the people on the team hadn't thought beyond their somewhat insulated groups in a long time. This was because they were extremely focused on driving their particular research projects and on competing with the other research groups for recognition and funding.

During the leadership training, what really catalyzed lasting change was how individuals, who were usually pitted against each other, were able to discuss calmly all the angles their new leader should see. They ended up talking about the entire enterprise and discovered that they all shared similar values and longer-term goals. It was a real eureka moment!

But before any of that new, positive capital could have a longer-term effect, it fell to Ellen to act as coach and mentor. She was either going to step up or miss the mark. This meant she had to learn to integrate all of that brilliant talent with the strategic direction of her organization. It meant she had to find new sources of funding for the research her scientists would conduct in the future. She had to position things so that everyone across the enterprise was valued equally. Also, she had to change the culture so that no one perspective or no one person was superior to another, even though all the scientists in her organization were prone to look at the world in a way that was in their own best interests.

Now it was up to Ellen to do exactly what she had just asked her people to do. She chose to step up and seize the opportunity to get to know each person well enough to initiate dialogues and relationships that would end up lasting well beyond the time she led that group. She made lifelong connections. As a result of building these bonds, Ellen matched the current capability of her staff to the strategic direction of the enterprise. She worked to help people from different disciplines find ways to work together. She didn't impose her ideas. Instead, she shared the dilemma and asked the team to create solutions and seize opportunities for improvement. In attending to the human element, she realized great success in magnifying the talent of her team.

Leaders like Ellen are effective because they show their people they care by connecting with them, and they help their people connect with each other. Furthermore, they help their people connect to being their best. To elevate their people, they use the best leadership and management techniques from science and industry to help their employees reach peak performance. For starters, they help workers match strengths to challenges and enable them to stay in constant learning mode. When people are in constant learning mode, they are always open to being coached and mentored. They realize that maybe they don't know everything about the right way to do their job. They are willing to get out of their comfort zones.

In addition to helping her people adopt this way of being, Ellen herself stayed in constant learning mode. She had come from the trenches and, like the scientists she now managed, she had her own position and point of view on things, including strategy, research, and fairness. However, she realized that she had to model the open-mindedness that she was asking of the people who reported to her.

The amount of effort it took to integrate the talents of her people was enormous. Ellen was modeling being an integrator and a total systems thinker for her people, even though she had come up through the ranks herself as a research scientist and knew what it was like to scrap for scarce research funding and compete with peers for publications in top refereed journals, plus garner recognition within the scientific community.

Funding for the traditional way of designing and conducting research was drying up, and Ellen's folks were trying to protect the current research dollars and associated talent as their own. However, Ellen got people to start thinking that funding and capability were owned by the entire enterprise, not by individuals or insulated groups. This way of thinking was outside their comfort zones, but they were willing to experiment with new approaches because Ellen had taken the time to build bonds with them. When it was all said and done, she helped them become total systems thinkers, and this resulted in more research funding for everybody. Thus modeling and mentoring were very important to Ellen's success as an effective leader.

Learning to appreciate the total system excited Ellen's people who were motivated by the chance to contribute their smart ideas and do great work. In putting forth their newfound total systems mindset, many of them had measurable and positive impacts across the organization. As an effective leader, Ellen also elevated her teams to collaborate around work assignments and grab the vision and run with it on the energy of possibility. Her leadership legacy lived on even after she was promoted to higher levels within her agency.

There are many leaders in government who have opportunities, like Ellen did, to create eureka moments that make a positive difference in their workforces. They have all the ability to make it happen if they choose to learn and use the tools and techniques of effective leadership. However, they will have to do it in a changing landscape.

## THE WORKPLACE HAS CHANGED

When nobody was looking, the landscape of work evolved radically. With technological advances over the past few decades, the nature of white-collar work has become extremely complex, requiring people and systems to be highly interdependent. This new environment requires work integration, meaning that individuals and groups cannot work separately or on discrete tasks. For the old way of work, people could work in silos or assembly lines. Now, people work in a total system and not in isolation. Whatever they do has ripple effects on everyone else. When one person doesn't make a deadline or a key supplier doesn't provide something on time, the ripple effect spans organizational boundaries.

In today's complex systems, leaders have to rewrite their playbooks because the impact of everybody's effort, competency, behavior, and attitude is enormous. We're now asking employees who used to be three levels down, and who used to care only about their own work, to be advocates for the entire enterprise. That's radically different. Also, there is the need for people to use common processes, such as shared calendars and master schedules to integrate work across organizational boundaries.

This is not a workplace with humanity in mind. It's a workplace with the enterprise in mind, and that's a problem unless leaders change their game plan to the plan that gets it all. The plan that gets it all requires managing the polarity of putting both the human element *and* the total enterprise at the forefront of strategy and daily actions. Over the years, my colleagues and I have helped many leaders realize that they can have it all, but first they need a holistic plan that paves a way for sustainable change and improvement.

But in many ways, change and improvement have a bad rap, which is one reason why leading an organization today is a daunting prospect. This is because change and improvement are not often implemented with the human element in mind, and even when they are, it's artificial. Consider managing conflict inside a large system. Managing agreements and conflicts with peers across organizational boundaries, with outside stakeholders, and within your team, is a foundational expectation of the twenty-first-century organization leader.

Yet many leaders avoid conflict and do not take the time or energy to change and improve the way conflict is managed within their enterprises. Also, the average employee rarely hears an articulation of what's possible when they come to work every day. Instead, they hear what's wrong from their customers, both internal and external. As a result, they yearn for encouragement. Many people don't perform because they don't have a good match between their talent and their work. Yet these same people want their skills to fit their jobs, and they want to be their best and do great things at work.

When we look around government agencies, we see things that appear to need a fix, such as the need for people to be encouraged and to be a good fit for their job assignments. However, in today's workplace, fix-it efforts are hard to sustain. That's because a fix-it trajectory has to keep finding negative things to fix. When fixing faults becomes part of an organization's culture, it can quickly run amok, draining energy from the best contributors. It rewards a negative focus and demotivates bright stars. Energy is drained from work life just when the group dynamic should be energized by its efforts. Fixing faults can become a formidable obstacle to the change we wanted in the first place. Instead, leaders need to help people rediscover their energy and vitality by seizing opportunities instead of getting dragged down by fault finding.

Today's federal leadership community needs a way ahead to breathe life back into the human element. Leaders want and need tools to improve planning, implementation, and measurement of the human capital front and to help their people thrive. They are eager to set goals for improvement and achieve great results in this most important area. Leaders realize it's their job to do this, and they want to do it with excellence.

Government leaders want to energize their people (including employees and contractors) and help them leverage imagination and innovation. They want to hire and integrate great people who are committed to the mission and who infuse the culture with sizzling vitality. And they want to unleash a magic dynamic within their organization as they create solid relationships, powerful communication, and genuine inspiration.

But, ultimately, it's about a shift in perspective and action. It's not just saying you're going to be a leader who is aware of the human element as people have done with so many quick-fix programs that have come and gone. This shift in perspective relies upon vision, because performance improvement efforts will go nowhere without shared vision. Leaders must create a collective vision with which people are willing to align themselves. The vision I'm talking about can be for a team, a business unit, or enterprise-wide. Implementing this vision requires hard work, tools, and commitment to creating a plan that gets it all.

Dee Hock, the former head of VISA, distilled it when he said, "In the field of group endeavor, you will see incredible events in which the group performs far beyond the sum of its individual talents. It happens in the symphony, in the ballet, in the theater, in sports, and equally in business. It is easy to recognize and impossible to define. It is a mystique. It cannot be achieved without immense effort, training and cooperation. But training and cooperation alone rarely create it."[1] The mystical "it" that Hock credits for virtuoso performance is the essence of the human element. Leaders must be in tune with the human element to bring into being the vision alignment necessary to drive peak performance of individuals, teams, and the entire enterprise.

## EFFECTIVE LEADERS MAGNIFY BRIGHT LIGHTS

Imagine you are a person being managed by an effective leader. As you interact, this leader makes you feel bigger than you felt before your conversation. This leader magnifies you. You might start the conversation seeing yourself in a 5 × 7 photo frame, but after talking with a masterful leader, you see yourself in an 8 × 10 frame—or larger. That's how my colleague Vaughan Limbrick[2] describes effective leadership. It comes down to helping everyone shine brighter. Even though you're a leader, it's not all about you. Instead, it's about doing what's best for people, not what's easiest for you. It's about encouraging people to achieve more than what they believe is possible. It's about inspiring folks to question and overcome their doubts. And it's about paying special attention to people's personal needs for achievement and development as you show them caring, compassion, and empathy.

Effective leaders also get groups to function better by adjusting the match between people and their work. The person who does well is the person whose strengths match the job assignments. The people who come early, stay late, and won't complain about the money are the ones who find joy in their work and are a good match. The effective leader is one who goes to the trouble of figuring out what it means to match people with job demands, to match people with their coworkers, and to match them with the organization itself. By figuring out these things, they build compatibility between individuals and the work environment, and research shows that the better the fit, the better the performance.

Implementing human capital strategies takes clarity, commitment, and energy. There's the plan, and there's the rollout. These happen in different ways, but what's the same across the board, and what determines the success or failure of the whole effort, is the leader's willingness to communicate. This means communicating not only the plan but also every step along the way. That's how an effective leader does exactly what he or she is supposed to do. The leader's role is to influence a diverse group of people to come together and execute a whole vision, one step at a time.

As part of the leader's communication mindset, he or she must realize that people respond not to the world as the leader sees it, but to the world as they see it. Effective communication (including face-to-face and in memos, meetings, emails, texts, and social media) starts with hearing and understanding rather than sending messages and trying to convince people of your point of view. As a leader, the more you know about your people, the more effective you will be in communicating with them. Remember, until and unless your message is heard, understood, and embraced by the people you are trying to reach, it is just noise to them.

This leads to another crucial idea that effective leaders embrace. Although styles range greatly, what effective leaders all do, in their own ways, is see possibility and broker hope. Even in an emerging leader, there is a sense of what makes the person in front of them tick and how to work with that. This makes them possibility thinkers. They see each person as a possibility and use dialogue to create a heart-to-heart bond. They create bonds with their employees, their supervisors, their suppliers, and their customers. This means they build bonds with all stakeholders of the enterprise. And they take advantage of every interaction to strengthen these bonds.

## FEDERAL LEADERS CAN HAVE IT ALL

Government executives can create a plan that maximizes all resources, including their people. Insightful government leaders realize that something must give for the human capital front to thrive in federal agencies. They understand they need to take care of their people, and they know it's the right and moral thing to do. However, there's more to it than that. Leaders who take care of their people are laying the foundation for those individuals to create desired business results throughout the organization. As important as this is in the commercial sector, it's equally important in government.

But I'm not just talking about giving lip service to the human element. I'm talking about tried and proven techniques from science and industry. Using these tools and techniques, leaders shift from looking at people as "capital" to knowing them as individuals, understanding their perceptions of where the enterprise is headed, and comprehending their feelings of alignment with the organization's direction.

This shift toward knowing, understanding, and comprehending the essence of your agency's workforce is critical. Federal leaders of the twenty-first century must be vision shapers and possibility thinkers. This means you exhibit the kind of energy that feeds the spirit. You encourage, voice possibilities, and model a high level of emotional intelligence. You help people seize opportunities, because seizing opportunities is the way to inspire, welcome, foster, and sustain change in your enterprise. When you try this on as a new way of being, you will be wielding a creation approach, not a fix-it approach, and you will be more effective as a leader. This is because your people will be more interested and better armed to seize opportunities that improve themselves and the enterprise.

Finally, for the impact of a leader to be enduring, no one can fake it. Leadership must be authentic to inspire people to take the risks involved in changing course. Success as a government leader relies on making the choice to evolve every day toward higher levels of ability. I'm not talking about getting an A+ in class or breaking a habit or getting a makeover. Classes end, habits can be forgotten, makeovers come undone. But the challenges of leadership continue unabated.

You cannot allow yourself to fall prey to the crush of daily work and undermine the best way you have to improve performance, which is working with the resources you already have. And your greatest resource is your people. If you choose to learn the techniques I'm offering you in this book, you can move your organization forward, even in the face of your daily challenges.

Initiating ongoing organizational excellence demands that you lead with spirit and choose to build momentum that achieves not just success in the near future but also sustained success, year after year. It's about embedding leadership deeply throughout the enterprise, and it requires a different way of thinking, speaking, and acting that comes from the heart. It's about helping people approach change.

People in most federal organizations are willing to change, and everyone is ready for some degree of change, even if it's very small. At the same time, people fear the consequences of change and what they might lose during and after a change. In fact, one of the natural polarities of being human is to want something and to fear it simultaneously.

## EVERYBODY WANTS TO GO TO HEAVEN, BUT NOBODY WANTS TO DIE

What I'm talking about is approach versus avoidance. It reminds me of the line from the old country music song that's the same as the heading for this section. "Approach-avoidance conflicts occur when there is one goal that has both positive and negative effects that make the goal appealing and unappealing simultaneously."[3]

For example, marriage has both positive and negative aspects. Positive aspects of marriage that we include are togetherness, sharing memories, and companionship. However, there are negative aspects that we avoid, including money, fidelity, and arguments. The negatives influence the decision maker to avoid the goal, while the positives influence him or her to approach the goal. The influences of the negative and positive aspects create a conflict because the decision maker either has to proceed toward the goal or not.

To continue with the example of marriage, a person might approach proposing to a partner with excitement because of the positive aspects of marriage: having a lifelong companion, sharing responsibilities. On the other hand, he or she might avoid proposing due to the negative aspects of marriage: arguments, money issues, joint decision making. It's easy to start toward the goal, but as the goal is approached the negative factors increase in strength, which causes indecision. If there are competing feelings about a goal, the stronger feeling will triumph.

In the federal workplace, while they may be a bit tentative, most employees and contractors are ready to approach change, and they yearn to rise to the occasion of achieving improvement goals. However, they may be hesitant because they're waiting for leadership to pay attention, show compassion, or inspire a real and specific pathway to success. This is because people naturally fear what they might lose during and after a change. It's the leader's job to help them embrace a plan that gets it all. This is a plan that drives change and at the same time lets people gain new, positive opportunities without losing anything except the roadblocks that were holding them back from winning with purpose and shining their brightest.

Leaders must understand that it's human nature for everyone to experience the approach-avoidance conflict when faced with the opportunity to improve the status quo. Effective leaders find ways to make the goal of change more attractive than the fear of change to their people and to themselves. Leaders who understand that approach-avoidance is natural can embrace it head-on and choose to experiment with behaviors that will catapult them and their workforce to the "heaven" I call measurable and sustainable improvement.

## YOU CAN BECOME A MORE EFFECTIVE LEADER

One behavior that I recommend experimenting with is walking around. This is a way to connect with others, but some leaders have a hard time doing it. Walking around is a leadership practice associated with the advanced social skills expected of leaders.

When employees see a leader routinely walking around, listening, and being available and open, they see a leader in motion and they want to help that leader succeed. Walking around is a way for leaders to bond with employees and communicate one-on-one with all levels of a group. Oddly, many leaders postpone walking around and being available to talk to staff. They consider it a luxury and feel as though they don't have time for it. Most leaders agree that walking around can have a powerful impact, but almost as many make excuses or put it off. I suggest that you don't put off walking around or connecting with your people. By doing so, you're denying yourself the opportunity to have it all.

Now more than ever, it's time to walk around and be with your employees and contractors to understand their situations and offer them real frontline solutions. If you are one of our nation's tireless public servants tasked with leading the way, you need to know the best proven practices that will help your people and your organization to thrive. All government leaders can adopt behaviors, such as management by walking around, that they can apply without spending beyond their means. Committed to excellence, all agency executives deserve to know how to keep their workforces happy and productive in the face of cost cuts, spending caps, and mandatory furloughs.

In this book, you're going to learn how to have a measurably powerful impact on your organization's productivity and performance. You will gain new confidence that big outcomes are waiting to be created in your enterprise right now. The research and experience that I'm sharing with you will boost your leadership effectiveness and revitalize your own innovative confidence.

Many leaders these days have gotten distracted from attending to the human element. Have you? Ask yourself: Do I know how to build energy into my enterprise, no matter how big or how lumbering it has been to date? If not, you can embrace a new mindset with a commitment to energizing your enterprise, because these days, energy is synonymous with sustainability. The upcoming pages cast a spotlight on what happens after the latest research and possibility thinking have been incorporated into time-tested methods. This book is based on research and practice that will push you to seize opportunities, invest your energy, and create sustainable results.

Some leaders share a secret. They have a discipline to find their best options by learning what it takes to lift their people to new heights. I'm here to help you adopt a discipline to lift your organization's human potential as high as you choose to lift it. Better yet, I'm going to help you free everybody in your organization to do the same. In this way, you can make it everybody's business to energize your enterprise.

In the upcoming chapters, I'll show you how to take your leadership effectiveness to the next level if you're willing to open your heart, walk around, and step outside your comfort zone. I'll demonstrate how to expand your imagination, creativity, and innovation. I'll explain how to best manage stress, time, and data. I'll teach you how to encourage, inspire, and mentor people to help them flourish. I'll guide you to engage people and boost performance at the individual, team, and enterprise levels.

In addition, you'll learn how to hire people who are a great fit. You'll discover how to help new people feel as welcome as possible. You'll come to understand how to build strong commitment in every individual on your team. You'll master how to make sure that values are a priority and how to exercise fairness so that people trust you and your motives. You'll adopt a discipline for attending to people's well-being and creating a supportive environment. You'll build strong relationships and motivate your people to succeed.

I'll illustrate how to communicate impeccably and adjust your communication style to meet your people's needs and recognize strengths that are different from your own. When this happens, you will have embraced an expanded view of diversity (not just gender, race, and age) and what's on the inside where the spirit lives—including individual dreams, strengths, and passions. Outlandish? Too good to be true? Well, it isn't. Effective leaders can do all of this and more!

## TOMORROW'S LEADERS WILL LIFT AND ENERGIZE THEIR PEOPLE

When leaders consciously attend to individuals' needs for development and communicate a compelling plan of action, their people will step forward with clarity, commitment, and energy to make it happen. Federal leaders—at every level—can adjust their mental stances, calibrate their hearts, and tap into their full leadership potential. Experience and research show that great solutions to organizational problems start with leaders who inspire trust and communicate effectively. The more fully employees are aware of an organization's direction, the more they will align their own choices with that direction.

Tomorrow's great leaders will make choices that guide the energy around them in a common direction. Change will be communicated by the way the leader leads. As they make better choices, leaders will be conscious— of themselves, their relationships, and their enterprises. They will cultivate consciousness, which is far more than understanding one person or one process. It's a state of being, a way of life.

Leaders' choices will determine our government's future. Despite their far-reaching impact, these choices will often play out as mundane daily decisions. Consider how small courtesies create lasting goodwill among colleagues. A person can become a powerful catalyst and emerge as a leader simply by developing the habit of asking others if they need help and, if they do, providing it. A simple "thank you" can punctuate the daily momentum with an important moment of conscious recognition, enriching the bonds on which we rely for enterprise success. In the same way, seemingly small individual choices will bring great visions into reality for the sustainable success of government agencies.

By the time you've read this book, you're going to find yourself with new leadership skills to uplift your people and identify affordable steps toward a leaner, faster, smarter, and happier enterprise. You will be able to implement the very best practices to help you optimize fit, onboarding, values, fairness, alignment, motivation, environment, well-being, relationships, and communication. I'm going to help you become the best leader you can be, do great things for your people, have meaningful professional success, and achieve your enterprise transformation goals.

The path to high-performing government enterprises is one where leaders demonstrably care about their employees and contractors. On this path, the leader's every thought, word, and deed counts. Meaningful leadership is driven to fruition by thinking, speaking, and acting from the heart as a catalyst for results. In the next chapter, we'll examine leadership rules that will help you elevate the human element and propel your organization to its next level of performance by creating connections with your people, helping them connect with each other, and helping them be their very best as partners in enterprise improvement.

## QUESTIONS FOR REFLECTION, DISCUSSION, AND ACTION

1. What are we doing to create (or maintain) a collective vision with which our people are aligned?

2. Do our people feel bigger and better after conversations with our leaders?

3. How effective are we at matching our people to their work? How do we know?

4. How effective are we at hearing and understanding our people? What are they telling us?

5. How do we build bonds with all our stakeholders?

6. Why would our people approach (or be attracted to) improving our enterprise, and why would they avoid (or be fearful of) improvement?

7. How often do our leaders "walk around"? What is the right frequency?

# LEADERSHIP RULES AND WISDOM TO LIFT YOUR PEOPLE

## PRINCE RICHARD LEARNS TO LEAD

There was once a young prince named Richard who wanted more than anything to be brave, wise, and joyful. In his childhood he was all these things, but as he grew older something happened to his brave, wise, and joyful spirit. He could never really put his finger on what caused him to change for the worse. Maybe it was a lot of little things over time. In any case, he began to see that he was neither brave nor wise, and he certainly wasn't joyful.

As he grew older, Prince Richard's contributions to those around him became less valuable. His respect for himself and others was unclear and conditional. He communicated poorly, was often unsupportive, had a hard time maintaining confidentiality, and did not effectively manage his agreements with others. He was somewhat conscious of his own bad behaviors, and he realized at some level that he had problems in dealing with people. From the outside looking in, he was undeniably a prince in trouble because his people did not look at him as their future leader or as someone who could effectively influence them.

Prince Richard's inner demons would appear just when he was about to have a positive impact on others. When he would start to teach a concept, act as an expert, aid others in solving a problem, or just show up in his role as the prince, his buttons would unexpectedly get pushed by the people he was trying to help or lead. Then, he would act in a way that alienated everyone.

For example, when the prince went on a tour with his kingdom's Royal Navy, things went terribly wrong. Officers and crew witnessed the prince's surreal and humiliating display of personal degradation of the enlisted troops one day as they were on deployment at sea. The prince was in his chair on the bridge observing the regular activities on deck. Suddenly, he did not like what he saw of the deck crew, jumped out of his chair screaming, went out on the bridge wing, and yelled at the crew for five minutes. Everyone stopped what they were doing, stood there, and weathered the outburst. In that incident, the prince berated the officer and demoralized his troops for a minor issue.

He acted like this because he thought others were observing him to see how the crew responded to him, and he just wanted to show them he was a tough leader and fit to be king. But he bypassed the chain of command (he had plenty of officers that he could have asked to deal with the crew), micromanaged the situation, was irrational in his assessment of the severity of the issue, went completely overboard in his emotional outburst, and personally humiliated his subjects in public for all to see. He set a poor example for current and future leaders, used fear and intimidation tactics, and lessened the effectiveness of the crew for the remainder of the tour. It was most unfortunate.

As you might expect, the prince would later realize what he had done and regret it. Each time an incident like this occurred, he ended up feeling worse about himself than ever. Sadly, the prince would one day be king, and this was no way for a future king to behave.

When the prince was at a particularly low point and feeling sad about his lack of effectiveness, a wise sage named Christopher visited the kingdom.

Christopher was preceded by a mighty reputation. Folks claimed he had helped many kingdoms become more prosperous and successful. Christopher was reputed to make people wiser, happier, and healthier. There was much mystery around him. Many people also feared him because those who had experienced his mentoring said that he pushed them outside their comfort zones.

Within days of Christopher's arrival in the kingdom, the prince invited him to the palace. By this time, Prince Richard was desperate and willing to do anything to change his current state. The prince pleaded with Christopher to help him once again be whole and to rediscover his brave, wise, and joyful spirit. Even if it required getting out of his comfort zone to change, Richard assured the sage that he was willing to pay the price. His intention was to become fit to lead his people.

Christopher agreed to help Prince Richard. Thus began many sessions, some long and some short, some in the day and some at night. Some were with the prince alone. Some included people in the prince's life (his father the king, his mother the queen, his subjects, and so on). The sessions with Christopher were based on a set of leadership rules. Although each of these rules made sense, it was a challenge to put them into practice consistently, especially without the right mindset. Thankfully, Christopher was a masterful coach and mentor.

The leadership rules that Christopher introduced were not esoteric, mysterious, or religious. They enhanced emotional intelligence, which is basically strong self-awareness and great interpersonal skills. They were self-evident and could easily be validated by any individual, including the prince. The rules were grounded in caring for one another. They were based on learning, growing, and taking risks. The rules promoted taking responsibility for self, relationships, and community. They were based on doing what was right in the moment and being accountable at the highest level.

According to Christopher, the rules helped leaders show their people they cared about them and helped leaders make every thought, word, and deed count. These rules helped leaders elevate the human element by creating connections with people, connecting them with each other, and helping them to be their very best. Christopher assured Richard that with the help of these leadership rules he could adjust his mental stance, calibrate his heart, and tap into his full leadership potential to inspire trust in all his people. Moreover, Christopher promised that Richard would be capable of guiding his people's energy in a common direction. Over the course of many days, Christopher led Prince Richard through an intensive study of the seven leadership rules in the following order.

## LEADERSHIP RULES

### 1. Create a Supportive Environment

Recognize, encourage, and help people who take risks. If people want to try a new way of doing things, for example, give them the chance to try it; if they succeed, recognize their success. If the new way fails, celebrate the lesson learned and encourage them to keep looking for ways to do things better. Really listen to what others are saying. Ask questions to clarify anything that you don't fully understand. Read the person's body language and respond appropriately. If the person looks hurt, ask if he or she feels bad about something and would like to talk about it. Invite people to participate as opposed to excluding them. Including and involving people is one true mark of a leader. Engage others by opening up more meetings to more people and pulling people into conversations that you might not normally pull them into. Taking actions like these to build a supportive environment will improve your organization's culture.

### 2. Maintain Confidentiality

Weigh carefully the potential consequences of quoting other people and spreading gossip. This means guarding against attribution and retribution. First, attributing statements to others out of context can be misleading. When you hold meetings, ask folks not to attribute what particular individuals said in the meeting afterward. If they want to share something about the meeting with those who were not in attendance, ask them to keep it general without pointing any fingers at particular individuals. Second, remember that people who pay a price (receive retribution) for what they do or say will be shy about showing up as a whole person in the future. As you encourage your people to share their opinions and input, be careful not to punish them in any way after the fact if you don't agree with their suggestions or point of view. Maintaining confidentiality by guarding against attribution and retribution builds trust and puts people at ease to be creative, think outside the box, and get focused. Breaking confidentiality weakens trust and promotes fear and bad feelings. The choice is yours to create a culture of trust with the help of this leadership rule.

### 3. Stay Focused and Be Prepared

Define and understand what it means to be on purpose and how to remain there. It's easy to get distracted and discouraged by the million things in your life. But the way to really make things happen and achieve your goals is to clear your mind, pull together the tools you need, and fully embrace the situation at hand. For example, make sure you get enough sleep and that you aren't overscheduling yourself to the point that you can't pay attention. Don't make these same kinds of expectations that result in your people being sleepy, overbooked, and unable to show up rested and alert at all times. Every leader can do little things like this to ensure that he or she shows up 100 percent in the moment and that all members of the organization realize that they too are expected and encouraged to show up fully engaged.

### 4. Manage All Agreements

Your cumulative record of adherence to your commitments forms the essence of how others view you. So get clear on your commitments, make fewer of them, and keep the ones that you make. Seek to minimize the impact of any commitments you choose to break by informing others in advance that you will not keep the agreement. If this is not possible, acknowledge breakdowns as soon as possible after the fact. One example of an important agreement is time. How you manage your time agreements with your people is very important. If you set a meeting to start at 9 a.m. and you show up at 9:15 a.m., what message does that send to those in attendance? It says that the meeting and they are not really important to you. Let me be clear, this isn't about being on time for everything. I'm talking about managing your time agreements so that everyone's expectations are clear. For example, if you're a person who shows up late for everything, let people know that for you 9 a.m. means between 9 a.m. and 9:15 a.m. Let people know the nature of what time means to you, and seek to understand what time means to them. Beyond time, extend this type of management to every one of your agreements to build trust with all your people. As a leader, it's your responsibility to set a great example of managing all agreements, especially with respect to time. People will notice your behaviors and follow your lead.

## 5. Use Open, Honest, and Direct Communication

Say what you think and feel to the people you believe will benefit from your message. For example, I once tried to tell a younger colleague that our clients were responding negatively to his hairstyle, which was a long mullet with an even longer braided rattail. In the beginning I was so worried about hurting his feelings that I shared some vague feedback with him about impressions that left him confused and not knowing what I was trying to tell him. My message left him with the feeling that he needed to improve something about himself. But he didn't know what it was!

Practice being open: be clear, as opposed to sending hidden messages. If a person walks away from a conversation with you and asks, "What was he trying to tell me?" the whole conversation was a waste of time. Practice being honest: truthfully share your thoughts, ideas, and feelings. Although stretching the truth or telling a little white lie may be convenient, keeping track of untruths can be most distracting and cause leaders to lose focus. Practice being direct: share your message with the person it is intended for as opposed to telling someone you hope will pass it along. What's the point of telling everyone else what you really need to tell a particular individual? It's inefficient, and you run the risk of your message being transmitted incorrectly. As a leader, it's your job to be a role model for impeccable communication, and others will be influenced to do the same.

## 6. Hold a Proper Attitude for Learning

Remain open to, contribute to, and build upon new ideas. No matter what is said, keep open to the one-percent possibility that all ideas have value and that you can learn from them. Suspend judgment, seeking first to understand the message of the other person. Learning is not confined to childhood or to school but takes place throughout life and in a range of situations. Being open to the one-percent possibility of learning from everyone enhances social inclusion, active participation, and professional development. Effective leaders constantly seek to learn new things and encounter alternative beliefs, cultures, and values. When leaders stop doing this, their personal development stops too.

Embrace every opportunity you have to learn from others. This doesn't mean agreeing with them on everything. We can learn from many people with whom we have nothing in common. Learning from others helps us grow emotionally, keeps us from making mistakes, and can often help with our own decision making. The beauty of wanting to learn from others is that you will remain open and willing to listen, which, in return, will draw others toward you. This will also open many new doors and experiences. Not only that, you'll find that maintaining a proper attitude for learning will also make you an effective teacher. As well as learning from the experiences of others, you may also be in great demand by people who want to learn from you.

## 7. Be Self-Monitoring

View your behaviors and see how they play out. Continuously hold up the mirror to see your reflection. Then, make appropriate adjustments. This leadership rule is your reminder to continuously build your self-awareness.

It is also your reminder to monitor your adherence to the other six leadership rules. To practice self-monitoring, pretend you're holding up a video camera and filming your every thought, word, and deed. Pretend to play it back and watch yourself in action. Are you effectively communicating with people, supporting them, staying focused? If so, great! If not, you can choose new thoughts, words, and deeds.

Effective leadership is truly a choice, and it is about building trust. When leadership rules are broken repeatedly, trust is lost. When used as a tool for managing relationships, leadership rules build a foundation for long-term trust, and they can help transform your organization.

## TRANSFORMING THE KINGDOM

After mastering the leadership rules over considerable time and a lot of hard work, Prince Richard was fit to be king. He began teaching people to become leaders throughout the kingdom and built trust with everyone. The rules empowered people and made them more effective. Over time, leadership rules transformed every agency and supplier in the prince's kingdom.

For example, in one of the kingdom's eleven royal horse facilities that supplied all horses and riders for the Royal Pony Express Mail, leadership rules helped create an environment where supervisors inspired riders to increase on-time deliveries. At all levels, fear and deceit were replaced with courage and relentless pursuit of truth. All workers, from the stable director to the horse trainers to the stall sanitation workers, found that the practice of open, honest, and direct communication brought them to a new level of effectiveness. Previously, riders were slipping, sliding, and getting hurt because of too many horse droppings. The stable director let the stall sanitation workers know they needed to do a better job of cleaning up. This resulted in significantly fewer accidents. At first, it was hard to look people in the eye and speak one's truth in a supportive manner, but then it became the norm. This stable, which had once been on the verge of a shutdown due to poor performance, became recognized as a superstar. Leadership rules were part of this profound change.

Since its inception, the Kingdom Revenue Service (KRS) had developed a reputation for shoddy service. Cumbersome and complex tax laws, numerous inaccuracies in account information, lack of timeliness in processing tax returns, and unhelpful, unfriendly tax agents were a few of many problems. When first introduced to the leadership rules, the KRS commissioner and his leadership staff were skeptical, if not resistant. However, in a short time the power of leadership rules took hold. The KRS stopped the practice of barging into peoples' homes and demanding their piggy banks in the middle of the night. They also decided to open a welcome center where people could bring in their tax payments at a convenient time of day and enjoy a cup of complimentary tea. The language within the team began to reflect more consciousness and self-awareness. They spoke to each other and their customers in a more supportive way. Similarly, behaviors changed to reflect the team's newly formed commitment. They started managing their agreements to process returns in a timely manner. The KRS commissioner and his senior team went on to deploy the leadership rules to other functional and cross-functional teams throughout the organization, and performance improved across the KRS enterprise.

Due to unprecedented budget cuts, the Department of Kingdom Defense (DOKD) had been undergoing a series of restructuring efforts in an attempt to gain efficiencies. These reorganizations had taken their toll on the culture of the DOKD. Infighting and competition for scarce resources were at an all-time high. Senior DOKD military and civilian personnel were in react mode and sought only to protect the interests of their respective units, not to optimize the larger system. At lower levels, employees felt demoralized and fearful. The rumor mill was churning on overdrive, and heads were rolling, literally. This was creating quite the brain drain. But a few leaders started to talk to their people about the consequences of quoting other people and spreading gossip. They helped people understand that attributing statements to others out of context can be misleading. As people began practicing maintaining confidentiality, they began to trust each other more and, as a result, people became more comfortable and creative. Gradually, maintaining confidentiality and the other leadership rules were embraced by a scattering of groups and individuals throughout the DOKD. These champions spread the leadership rules to everyone within their realms of influence. After a time, as more and more people practiced the leadership rules, things changed for the better at the DOKD.

Leadership rules helped the candlestick maker, Crown Wax, which was one of the kingdom's most important manufacturing organizations, create a common measurement system and an approach for assessing results across different business units and down to different levels of work groups. The first rule they adopted with gusto was to be self-monitoring. As they started to hold up the mirror, they realized they could create many valuable mirrors, or metrics, to keep everyone informed of performance at all levels. Thanks to metrics, they began inspecting what was expected. By doing so, they realized they were putting wicks that were too short in all the candles. This meant there was an extra step in the production process to cut the candle and release the end of the wick so that it could be lit. Upon reflection, this obvious problem was fixed by procuring longer wicks. The extra step in the process was eliminated, and production increased by 25 percent

Finally, the kingdom's bread distributor, Grain of the Domain (GotD), successfully designed and implemented their "warehouse of the future" vision. With leadership rules as their guide, they asked Giuseppe, the warehouse worker, for suggestions on how to get the wagon drivers to eat less bread while they were delivering it. He suggested putting locks on the delivery wagons that could be opened only by the store owners at the point of delivery. Although Giuseppe's idea was outside the box, GotD leadership was open to the idea, and implemented it. As a result, distribution costs decreased by 30 percent. Believing in the one-percent possibility that every single employee can make a difference—and creating a supportive environment—propelled process-improvement teams, made up of all hourly employees, to lead the company in astronomical savings across all bread distribution centers.

Over the years, Christopher the sage became a celebrated and honored citizen and was even presented with the key to the kingdom. He worked with many individuals and groups, and the kingdom became one of the most prosperous in the land. Finally, the time came for Christopher to move on. You see, Christopher's purpose was not confined to this kingdom alone. This was one of many kingdoms he was destined to help. His commitment was to promote vitality and energy in as many places as possible.

Prince Richard, who had grown by leaps and bounds since Christopher's arrival, was frightened to hear of Christopher's pending departure. He requested a meeting with Christopher. As their meeting began, the prince made no pretense of his concern. He blurted out, "Christopher, what will I do without you? You never told me the secrets of leadership! No one can replace you! What about the people you have yet to touch? What will become of my kingdom?"

Christopher began to laugh and said, "I have done nothing but hold up a mirror for you. You and each individual I've worked with are perfectly capable of doing this for yourselves. You can also help others learn the skill."

"Then why is this your life's work, if it is so simple?" exclaimed the prince.

"I am committed to this work, and it is consistent with my purpose," answered Christopher. With that he smiled, said goodbye, and departed.

Christopher was not seen again in the kingdom, but the results of his actions lived on. The kingdom became more prosperous than ever, the prince became a great king, and all people eventually found it hard to believe that looking in the mirror and living by the leadership rules had ever been difficult for them to do.

## EFFECTIVE LEADERSHIP

I hope you've enjoyed my fantasy romp through Prince Richard's kingdom and that you might see some parallels within your own organization. With the proper sentiment, mindset, knowledge, and tools, leaders can empower multitudes of talented people to collectively bring about required change or to maintain needed stability, depending upon the situation and what is needed. Over the past twenty-plus years, I've had the opportunity to witness leaders bring about the change *and* maintain the stability that boosts enterprise-wide quality, speed, savings, and innovation. These results required leadership commitment, just as they did in Prince Richard's kingdom.

By adjusting your sentiment and mindset, you can cocreate a shared vision, attend to people's needs, and encourage everyone to achieve new heights during difficult times. To be a better steward of your workforce, you need to apply corrective strategies, close critical gaps, and evaluate desired results on the human capital front. You must conquer how to think and feel in new ways that make a positive difference for you, your people, and your enterprise.

As you adjust your sentiment and mindset, I challenge you to go beyond your current capabilities and convince others to push their limits. You can do it, and it will be fulfilling. The question is not "Why do it?" Instead it is "Why not?" If you are committed to going beyond your own limits and want the most for yourself and others, you have the choice to make it happen. Challenging yourself and others to experiment with new behaviors is part of effective leadership.

As the prince found, creating a culture that adheres to the leadership rules does not start with pushing others. Effective leadership starts with pushing yourself to become more conscious of your own strengths, weaknesses, and capabilities. Effective leadership means maintaining and managing your courage, clarity, power, and limitations in a way that promotes improvement, civility, and wisdom within yourself and your enterprise. It means living the leadership rules and serving as a role model for others to follow.

## Promote Happiness and Well-Being

For starters, effective leaders take actions that relieve sadness and ease anxiety in the workplace. An easy way to do this is to encourage people to take breaks throughout the day to move around. Movement can help people relieve the pressure or sadness they feel building up inside. During lunch breaks, encourage people to go outside for a walk, especially if they sit at a desk all day. Stretches and breathing exercises can also help them feel more calm and relaxed, and these can be easily taught and then done while folks are working. Or, if your work environment is filled with negative energy and stress, you can take quick steps to make things more positive. For example, surprise everyone and bring in a novel afternoon snack like popcorn or dried fruit (delicious and nutritious), which is a small but symbolic gesture that people will appreciate. It is little things like these that uplift the organization in difficult times, especially in an economic downturn.

## Tend to Your Talent

Another way to promote leadership rules is to inspire, recognize, and retain top talent. Employee engagement is at the heart of retaining good people and includes establishing clear goals for the enterprise and communicating them to everybody. Measurable goals motivate people, and when they achieve them, they feel a sense of accomplishment. Specific goals with measurable targets and timelines clarify what is expected of people. In general, people want to manage their agreements and achieve success. Once they embrace clear goals, they won't stop until they cross the finish line.

## Create Powerful Messages

Another way to implement leadership rules is to maximize communication. On the communication front, you can easily distribute frequent newsletters or email messages to communicate changes, expectations, and relevant announcements. This will keep everyone in the loop of what is going on in the office. In addition, with little effort, you can create a communication center for staff that allows everyone to share work-related information. Once it's established, encourage everybody to check the communication center often to stay current.

## Make Human Capital a Priority

Yet another way to roll out leadership rules is to help employees drive a human capital strategy that makes a difference. A central pillar in the strategic management of human capital is the alignment of human capital strategies with enterprise mission, goals, and objectives through analysis, planning, investment, and management of human capital programs. Human capital planning is how leadership designs a coherent framework of human capital policies, programs, and practices to achieve a shared vision integrated with the strategic plan of the enterprise. Implementation of a strategic human capital plan is a key step in building a highly effective, performance-based organization by recruiting, acquiring, motivating, and rewarding a high-performing, top-quality workforce. Your plan becomes the road map for continuous improvement and the framework for transforming your culture and operations.

Although the structure, content, and format of strategic human capital plans will vary, there are certain common elements that should be included. Your plan should contain a clearly understood strategic direction, customer and stakeholder human capital management outcomes, strategies for accomplishing the goals, an implementation plan, a communication playbook, and an accountability system.

## A Word to the Wise

But be warned. The happy and high-performing workplace described here is not achieved with a quick fix. It's driven by ways of thinking and feeling that activate leadership qualities in every person and reveal unrecognized leaders in the most unassuming workers. This requires a leader who can see and lead others as equals, partners, and allies. Not everyone thinks and feels this way, but everyone *can* think and feel this way, just like Prince Richard.

People who practice the leadership rules are able to draw out the potential of everyone so that each individual who contributes to the momentum of change and improvement is free to do so without reservation. Leaders who choose this path help everyone become part of a network in motion toward ever greater success, and they ensure that a sense of leadership and accomplishment are shared throughout the enterprise. They believe in a system of participation in which all people are free to contribute their best talent, knowledge, judgment, and skill. I hope you are (or choose to become) one of these leaders.

## HEART SMART LEADERS ENERGIZE THEIR WORKFORCES

It may sound silly, but the heart has a brain. As a leader, it's important to know this because great leaders are heart smart. Heart smart leaders are role models for honesty, empathy, communication, appreciation, and collaboration. They create a supportive environment, maintain confidentiality, and stay focused. They communicate impeccably, manage all agreements, hold a proper attitude for learning, and are always self-monitoring. Heart smart leaders embody the leadership rules, and they trust their hearts to help them make every thought, word, and deed count when they communicate with their people.

"Experiments conducted at the Institute of HeartMath have found remarkable evidence that the heart's electromagnetic field can transmit information between people. [They've] been able to measure an exchange of heart energy between individuals up to 5 feet apart. [They] have also found that one person's brain waves can actually synchronize to another person's heart. Furthermore, when an individual is generating a coherent heart rhythm, synchronization between that person's brain waves and another person's heartbeat is more likely to occur. These findings have intriguing implications, suggesting that individuals in a psychophysiologically coherent state become more aware of the information encoded in the heart fields of those around them."[1] Something to think about!

Yes, effective leadership requires a lot of intelligence and logical abilities, but it also requires making the heart connection with people. Stewards of every enterprise should want everybody to lead from the heart. That's because great leaders capture the hearts and minds of people who will make their best contributions when they're more than just employed—when they're inspired and fully engaged. Until change occurs in the heart, no workplace can resolve issues related to the human element. Change must happen in the heart and in habits, or it will be superficial, and old habits will slip back into place when the pressure is high and when a new and better way of working is most important.

My role as your coach is to enhance and build upon what's already in your heart and in your head so you can experiment with new behaviors that will inspire, motivate, and energize your workforce. Not only will my guidance raise you to your next level of leadership effectiveness, but it will also help you lift your people to higher peaks of productivity and satisfaction with thoughts, words, and deeds that drive workforce excellence.

It's your choice to tap into yourself to take action that will engage, inspire, and motivate your people. Doing so will be positively empowering and potentially transformative for you and your organization. Even if you face daunting and unpredictable conditions, you are the force to lift your people and organization to greater levels of possibility and performance. Tools like the leadership rules and other guidance for effective leadership that I've laid out in this chapter will elevate you as a leader and maximize your ability to make a meaningful difference in the lives of your people. In addition, there are a few foundational cornerstones on which I encourage you to rely.

## FOUNDATIONAL CORNERSTONES

Leaders who achieve meaningful success do three things:

- Imagine what others don't.
- Manage stress, time, and data.
- Inspire and encourage others.

These three foundational cornerstones will allow you to energize your workforce and to thrive as a leader. Another way to think about these cornerstones is that they are preliminary suppositions to effective leadership.

### Imagination, Creativity, and Innovation Create Opportunities

"Imagination is the ability to form new images and sensations that are not perceived through sight, hearing, or other senses. Imagination helps make knowledge applicable in solving problems and is fundamental to integrating experience and the learning process. It is a whole cycle of image formation, which is hidden as it takes place without anyone else's knowledge. People may imagine according to their moods, and it may be good or bad depending on the situation."[2] Imagination is the ability and process of inventing scenarios within the mind from elements derived from perceiving the world around us. Effective leaders create supportive environments that encourage all people across the enterprise to use their imaginations to create new possibilities.

Creativity is the process of producing something that is both original and worthwhile. In a summary of scientific research into creativity, Michael Mumford suggested: "Over the course of the last decade, however, we seem to have reached a general agreement that creativity involves the production of novel, useful products."[3] Creativity is a phenomenon whereby something new and valuable is generated (e.g., an idea, a joke, a literary work, a painting, a process, a solution). Effective leaders choose to fan the flames of creativity throughout their enterprises.

"Innovation is the application of new solutions that meet new requirements, inarticulate needs, or existing market needs. This is accomplished through more effective products, processes, services, technologies, or ideas that are readily available to markets, governments, and society. An innovation is something original, new," and important that gains a foothold in a market or society. "Innovation differs from invention in that innovation refers to the use of a better idea or method, whereas invention refers more directly to the creation of the idea or method itself. Innovation differs from improvement in that innovation refers to the notion of doing something different rather than doing the same thing better."[4] Effective leaders not only promote innovation, but also they reward and recognize it.

One of the greatest powers in the history of our nation has been our creative force, our ability to imagine possibilities, and our innovative strides. It's the foundation of our culture and our country and has led our nation to be a world leader in the areas of commerce, science, and technology. The same is possible for our future if people's full potential is unleashed, organizations are free to operate at full capacity, and initiatives are aligned with the goals of the enterprise. Otherwise, federal organizations could waste their greatest resource—human creativity. Creative innovation is one of our nation's most precious assets.

I'm excited to show you not only how leadership is an art but also how effective leadership frees the work of others to evolve toward innovative heights. Leadership is not just a flowery exercise; it's a lot of work.

As you implement the leadership rules, you will want to choose a mental stance for effective leadership. Effective leaders choose to see problems not as obstacles but as exciting opportunities to be seized. In the federal workplace, these problems (or opportunities) include staff shortages, inflexible schedules, and temporary assignments that disrupt the balance between work and home life. These can all contribute to low morale if not addressed appropriately. The wise choice, I assert, is to see these *and* seize them as opportunities.

## People Respect Leaders Who Manage Stress, Time, and Data

Despite difficult pressures, effective leaders remain focused, clear, and calm, which builds the confidence of everyone around them. Due to the natural "fight or flight" response, certain instincts take over when people, including leaders, respond to stress. The faster you can identify your fight or flight response and avoid pumping unneeded adrenaline through your body, the more easily you'll be able to respond to the situation and to the people at hand.

As a leader, you must be able to override instinct in stressful work settings, or you'll end up feeding tension and fueling reactivity. You can learn to model for your people how to choose tools to reduce psychological stress so work proceeds in a constructive manner. Studies show that people who choose to meet stressors with a positive attitude develop a remarkable hardiness that allows them, despite stress, to stay committed, feel in control, and seek challenges. This hardiness is important for a healthy workplace, and it's one mark of effective leadership in federal agencies where stressors include budget cuts, hiring freezes, and increasing workloads.

Effective leadership takes time, but time is not the enemy of stellar leaders. Instead, it's a precious resource to be managed as carefully as any project that takes time to do right. Time should be managed with care, especially when you are committed to offsetting stress. The best way to use limited time is to become more efficient. Efficiency is a choice. More accurately, efficiency is a collection of hundreds of minor choices about how you behave from day to day.

Efficiency depends on a moment-to-moment conscious evolution in your behavior concerning time. As a leader, your time-management skills have a far-reaching collateral impact. By consciously respecting the use of time in the workplace, you are treating those around you as the precious resources they are. Time management for leaders is about respect for others, and managing time promotes the values and vision of your leadership.

Effective time management puts into action your commitment to ensure there is enough time, for example, to frame the right questions and get good answers, to walk around and listen, and to be open to new ideas. Time management modeled by leadership is especially important in the federal workplace, where time challenges are exacerbated by assignments that disrupt the balance between work and home life, inflexible schedules, and funding shortages.

Before implementing the leadership rules and pushing others to new levels of performance, successful leaders are already pushing themselves and won't settle for anything but the right information to guide and shape sound decisions. Leadership is about taking responsibility for measuring the right things and for measuring things right, not passing the buck down the line. Furthermore, leadership is first and foremost about polishing your own mindset and behaviors. It's about looking in the mirror every day to monitor if you are living the leadership rules to which you've committed.

## Encouragement, Inspiration, and Mentoring Help People Flourish

Another way to embed leadership rules within your enterprise is to get everyone involved. Start encouraging folks to achieve more than what's thought possible by setting high and realistic standards and through ongoing discussions to keep those standards on everyone's radar. Make it your mission to inspire folks to question their own commonly held assumptions; think for themselves; reframe problems; and approach matters in innovative, collaborative ways. Experiment with paying focused attention to people's personal needs for achievement and development. Look at your reflection, not out the window, to take responsibility for poor outcomes, never blaming other people, external forces, or bad luck. When great things happen, go ahead and give others the credit. You'll be glad you did.

Act as a caring, compassionate, and empathetic mentor. Agencies that have the highest-ranking workforce satisfaction ratings have top leaders who listen and work on resolving matters that cause employee stress and unhappiness. Like these leaders, you can achieve more meaningful leadership outcomes by thinking, speaking, and acting from the heart as a catalyst for results at all levels. When you are doing your best, it inspires the people in your organizations to do their best.

## NOW THAT YOU'RE IN MOTION, THERE'S MORE

Like Prince Richard, you and every leader in every government agency or organization can be exceptional leaders as you put the leadership rules and foundational cornerstones in place. You can model and teach them to everybody in your organization. This will lift your people to new heights. Now that you're in motion, are you ready to take more action? If so, let's next take a look at some specific tools and methods that you can use to energize performance throughout your organization. You will experiment with hiring people who are a good fit, helping new people feel welcome, and building strong commitments throughout your enterprise. You will make sure that your organization's culture is great by making values a priority, increasing perceptions of fairness, and attending to people's well-being. You will create a better work environment by helping your people build strong relationships, communicate impeccably, and seize the success they want and deserve. Finally, you will understand and benchmark your own choices and results compared to those of our government's greatest leaders.

## QUESTIONS FOR REFLECTION, DISCUSSION, AND ACTION

1. What are our "leadership rules," and how do we model them?

2. How do we hold up the mirror for ourselves to examine our leadership effectiveness?

3. How do we promote the happiness and well-being of our people? How are we doing?

4. How do we manage our communication front? Where are we strongest? What is our biggest opportunity to improve communication?

5. What are the signs that we make human capital a priority in our organization?

6. Are we engaging, inspiring, and motivating our people? How do we know?

7. How are we managing
   - Imagination, creativity, and innovation?
   - Stress, time, and data?
   - Encouragement, inspiration, and motivation?

# PART

## 3

# THE SOLUTION

# ENGAGE YOUR SUPERSTAR STAFF:
# FIT, ONBOARDING, AND COMMITMENT

## LOSING VIVIAN

Many years ago, when I was an emerging leader working for a different company, I was part of a team that actively recruited a young and brilliant social scientist. Recruiting Vivian (a.k.a. Viv) took place over three years during which she completed multiple internships. When Viv was ready to graduate with her PhD, the organization made her a great offer and she joined the team. When Viv first came aboard, there was a honeymoon period when everything was great. But, in less than a year, this superstar in whom the company had invested so much time and energy in recruiting gave her two-week notice. Everyone was shocked, devastated, and even a bit hurt.

During Viv's exit interview, she shared that she had not expected to spend so much time in solitude. She had expected to have constant interaction with her teammates. This was enlightening! The organization had set Viv up to work from a home office when she wasn't working with clients. That was the organization's culture, but no one had realized that this hadn't been revealed to Viv during her internships, when she worked on projects in an office near a client. Someone was always in the office to work with her and give her enriching developmental experiences. Viv's internships had not been a realistic preview of the job that she was offered. In the end, because her expectations weren't met, Viv walked away. The organization suffered the loss of a superstar and incurred the expense of recruiting a replacement.

## WHY ENSURING THE RIGHT FIT, EFFECTIVE ONBOARDING, AND TRUE COMMITMENT OF SUPERSTARS IS SO HARD

Every leader would love for great people to be beating down their doors to come to work for them, stay long term, and make a meaningful contribution to the organization during their entire tenure. But how do you hire the best people, get them integrated, and make sure they're committed from the get-go? It isn't easy, and there are many challenges.

### Problems with Attracting Talent That's the Right Fit

Many organizations attract people who can't or won't deliver great results. It's often because the organization isn't delivering great results. People are attracted to what's similar to them and what's comfortable. If no one in the organization is in tune with what the organization is about, and they radiate negative energy about the organization wherever they go, that does one of two things: It either repels great people or attracts not-so-great people. If people don't like what they do at work and are not having fun doing it, they talk about it all the time, and that creates bad publicity for the organization. If an organization is not a great place to work, people can sense it. If this is the case, it's up to people in the organization to fix this problem.

### Problems with Ensuring Effective Onboarding

Many organizations don't ask people what areas they want to develop in and what their time frame is for that development. Many leaders fail to take an interest in their people's career paths and what's important to them. Job variety and job autonomy are lacking, and mentoring is missing in many work settings. Often, we see an employee being paid to go to a weeklong conference or given tuition assistance, but it's disconnected and develops individual skills that aren't aligned with the organization's mission. Many leaders and managers don't model the behaviors and attitudes they expect to see from their people. The budget for learning and development is not well thought through or fairly distributed in many organizations.

Moreover, the old way of onboarding people is to go through a one-day orientation program that's data heavy. Then somewhere along the line, you get an employee handbook. You learn and retain almost nothing. Some organizations do a "dump and run." "Here's the computer, your business cards . . ." That's not adequate. This doesn't make people comfortable or enhance their chance for success. Therefore, it doesn't enhance the company's chance for success. There needs to be a planned introduction and sharing of knowledge.

You can ignore people, throw them into the system, and let them figure it out. This has varying degrees of effectiveness. Or you can use structured indoctrination. For instance, some organizations construct a weeklong boot camp that's fairly structured and offered when necessary, based on influx. This method can be effective. Some organizations assign buddies, a go-to person for onboarding to teach folks about internal operations and customer delivery, which can work well.

A colleague recalls one job where she received a form listing all the people she needed to meet, and those people were supposed to sign off on the form as she met them. She went around and met people, but no one bothered to help her find out where the people were or how to best reach them. No one asked if she was making progress. They did not facilitate the process well. She soon realized it was just paperwork, and since she had other tasks to work on, she never finished it.

Productivity drain; underusing newcomers as a source of fresh, new ideas; and retaining employees long enough to justify the costs of recruiting, hiring, and training them: These are challenges in onboarding employees. Scientists conducted an interesting study on getting new hires up to speed quickly. They found that "in today's volatile economy, more than 25 percent of all workers in the United States have been with their company less than a year and more than 33 percent less than two years. Americans will, on average, change jobs 10 times between the ages of 18 and 37."[1] Moreover, "lost productivity resulting from the learning curve for new hires and transfers [accounts for] between 1 percent and 2.5 percent of total revenues. On average, the time for new hires to achieve full productivity ranges from eight weeks for clerical jobs to 20 weeks for professionals to more than 26 weeks for executives."[2]

Finally, "45 percent of companies estimate the turnover costs to replace and train a lost employee at more than $10,000."[3] Only part of this can be attributed to the employee. Some fault lies with the organization.

## Problems with Making Sure Your Staff Is Truly Committed

When organizations don't develop people, those people look for opportunities somewhere else. However, many organizations fail to create opportunities for people to grow and develop at a pace that's important to them. Many leaders are not transparent about the strategy of the organization, how it's changing, and how people are a part of the change. In many organizations, no one listens to people and they have few or no forums in which to communicate their ideas.

In many work settings, employees don't believe or feel they can take a problem to whatever level they need to get it resolved. Or they don't think they have permission to solve the problem themselves. This decreases their sense of control over their destiny. Many organizations have arbitrary rules that are not explained well. A lot of organizations don't bother to explain why things came to be; as a result, people don't follow the rules. If leaders don't explain to employees why constraints exist, they don't see how it adds value and think it's an arbitrary rule to harass or inconvenience them.

Leaders also contribute to employee burnout by using someone to the absolute max, making it impossible for him or her to keep up with new skills and knowledge. Even now, most manufacturing companies invest more money in maintaining their equipment than in maintaining their human capital. If obligations are not fulfilled, this can cause resentment. Unfulfilled obligations lead to a breakdown in trust. The breakdown is cumulative. Over time, employees and companies can build up baggage between each other that they may not resolve in a constructive fashion. These are a few of the challenges that contribute to people leaving instead of staying and thriving in many organizations.

In an un-energized enterprise, people throw up their hands and say, "I can't believe they didn't do what I thought they were going to do." Unfortunately, many unfulfilled obligations go unresolved. There was a leader in the government who knew there would be a reduction in the workforce. By law, he could not share details with employees. He avoided holding a Town Hall meeting to address workforce concern because he could not answer the many questions they might ask him. This was not ideal, but he waited until the law allowed him to tell them more. Only three people were laid off, but hundreds of people were in anguish from the process. As a result, a lot of trust was lost.

Many organizations don't deal with unmet expectations, at least not directly. They may be noted, but there is no conversation that results in anything productive. For example, we might think helping and pitching in is important, but we don't give the message that people are not doing that as often as they should. The feedback given in organizations is mainly focused on performance reviews, and these types of expectations are not generally written on that piece of paper. Managers don't often want to bring up that sort of expectation. There's no particular forum in most organizations to bring up expectations that are not part of the performance review process, and since it's uncomfortable, many people don't do it.

## HIRE SUPERSTARS WHO ARE A GREAT FIT

Employers must understand what it means to match people with job demands, to match people with their coworkers, and to match them with the organization itself. With this knowledge, organizations can build compatibility between individuals and the work environment. Research shows that the better the fit, the better the performance. It has everything to do with employee happiness, health, and performance.

As an organization, you should demonstrate the traits you want to hire in people. To get someone who can deliver great results, you have to demonstrate delivery of great results. Like-minded people will find you. If all people in the organization are so in tune with what the organization is about, and they radiate positive energy about the enterprise no matter where they are, that attracts people. When people like what they do and have fun doing it, they tell everybody about it.

People in an energized enterprise have an elevator speech that rolls off their tongues everywhere they go. Not too long ago my colleague's son told him, "I have no idea what you do, but you have so much fun I want to do it." Needless to say, my colleague has a great elevator speech. Keep your eyes open for people radiating in the work they're doing, and maybe you can convince them to radiate with you. Some are radiating in spite of being in un-energized enterprises. You might be able to convince them that your organization is a better fit.

It's wise to nurture pipelines of people once you find a good source. College recruiting is not just about recruiting new graduates. If you find a program that produces graduates aligned to the culture and mentality that you're looking for in your organization, go back to it. There may be something about the process they go through that is a more natural fit with your organization's culture.

Be a great place to work. If you want to attract people, be attractive. We've had many clients say "When I get out and retire, I want to come work for you." People can sense it because we take pride in what we do and we have fun doing it. Sometimes you're wrong as an organization and as a leader. Be willing to be honest and to admit when you're wrong. Be a place where people can trust that if something is not right, you will not ignore it. Be willing to look at the ugly and the beautiful and do something about it. Have some energy. Be so excited about what you do that all your employees are as excited as you are, and in turn they will become recruiters for your organization.

Research indicates that "recruiters who are selected for desired qualities (e.g., personableness) and trained to provide the correct information in a manner that is consistent and fair will likely be more successful, regardless of their organizational function, gender, or race. Perceptions of fit [are] one of the strongest predictors of attitudinal applicant attraction outcomes."[4]

## Fit with Job Demands

Many people are in jobs they loved two or three years ago. Now that they've learned the job, they want the next challenge, but the organization wants to keep them doing the current job. Matching people to jobs is about stretching their abilities, but not to the breaking point. Most people want a job that's a little harder than they think they can do. If it's too hard, they give up. If it's too easy, they get bored. The leader has to keep a tab on where everyone is on that rubber band of goal efficacy.

In one study, results supported a negative relation between both person-job fit and participative leadership with emotional exhaustion. This suggests that employees' ability to deal with emotional exhaustion is enhanced when they believe their supervisor consults with or considers them and when employees think that they have adequate personal capabilities to deal with work demands. Results also supported positive relationships between emotional exhaustion and organizational deviance and negative relationships between emotional exhaustion with job satisfaction and organizational commitment. The results have implications for selecting the right managers with the ability to inspire and motivate employees as well as selecting the right employees with the attitudes and skills that match job demands.[5]

For most people, fit is everything. If you're in a job you think you're not competent to perform or feel you're being underused, then you're going to be miserable, resentful, or both. In an energized enterprise, why wouldn't you want to use all your talent and employee capabilities? Exceptions might be cases where employees are suffering from long-term or short-term issues such as divorce, family death, substance abuse, nervous breakdown, or severe depression. Those cases are rare. The mindset or intention of great leaders is that everybody's capable. If employees are not performing as desired, then leadership is not maximizing or using the strengths of those employees.

In a heavily networked world, it's not smart to make enemies. Forced firing of an individual should be the last resort. What's the alternative if talent is no longer needed in an organization? The best course of action is the following approach:

1.  Explain the business argument that lists why there's no room for that capability in the current work flow.

2.  Acknowledge that business realities "change on a dime" and that you might need the individual's talent sometime in the future.

3.  Ask permission to keep in touch, and explore whether the individual may want to come back.

4.  Provide positive work references. Remember that you want departing employees to thrive in their new jobs, returning to you in the future with vastly improved competency and capability.

It starts at the interview. You want a true and accurate job description, not necessarily a complete job description. You explain, "We're looking for interdisciplinary talent. We're looking for you to bring ideas to us. We're looking for you to enhance the job." These are the types of discussions that help people grow.

Based on research findings, "teams and team leaders should ensure that team members' roles and abilities are aligned." Also, leaders should identify "individuals' personal growth and development priorities" before designing roles. Also, leaders should provide "accurate and informative performance feedback" to ensure individuals have correct perceptions of how they fit with their role.[6]

### Fit with Coworkers

It's important for people to understand their fit with a workgroup, but they don't have to all be friends or buddies. There can be an oddball, as long as there's a culture in place that values that person's individuality. Others honorably recognize he's quirky and value that quirkiness rather than ostracize it. To quote Jim Collins, it's all about "getting the right people on the bus and in the right seat."[7] You've got to have fit with at least a few coworkers. We're social creatures, and if we've got nobody for eight hours out of the day, we're going to be miserable.

Supervisor support is important because researchers Chien-Cheng Chen and Su-Fen Chiu have found that higher levels of supervisor support increase job satisfaction and person-organization fit, higher levels of job satisfaction and supervisor support increased organizational citizenship behaviors, and lower levels of job tension increased organizational citizenship behaviors.[8] Transformational leaders align people around an organizational vision by creating "fit" or congruence around goal importance, which directly affects the attitude and performance of the people around them.[9]

## Fit with the Organization

If there's no fit with employees' values and the organization's values, it's not going to work. People won't contribute. Displayed organizational values are what you actually see in people's behaviors. In this case, having no fit will certainly upset people. What you see every day is what people will react to. A lot of people are drawn to organizations whose values resonate with the values they have. In fact, research shows that people who are more committed and satisfied in their jobs are less likely to leave when there is fit between their individual moral levels and the ethics of their organization.[10]

Likewise, studies indicate that an organization's values can attract potential employees, but the values of recruiting organizations must be visible for that to happen. Potential applicants must be able to assess recruiting organizations' values. To do so, applicants must have proximity, exposure, and familiarity with the recruiting organization's values.[11]

Finally, Hilary Anger Elfenbein and Charles A. O'Reilly found that person-culture fit based on value congruence among team members moderates some of the negative effects of demographical differences. Person-group fit especially serves an ameliorative function for individuals whose demographic background puts them at risk for lower retention (including people of lower socio-economic status and ethnic minorities). Elfenbein and O'Reilly note that this is important for organizations trying to recruit and retain underrepresented groups.[12]

## Best Course of Action When There Is No Fit

Once you determine that someone is not a good fit for the organization or not good for the team, you can increase fit through culture-building interventions. These activities can help with improving or assessing fit. For example, many of our client organizations have costume parties, holiday activities, decorating, family picnics, and chili cook-offs.

The best course of action for an individual when there is no fit is to get a new job. Life is short. You go somewhere, show up as the person you are, and it gets received however it's received. If fit doesn't happen, then I encourage folks to get a new job. Find work you really want to do with people you want to work with for an organization you want to work for, and encourage others to do the same. Often after a bad experience, however, people have a distorted perception that their job is worse than it actually is.

My colleagues and I have met people who are miserable in their jobs. But when we look around, we think it doesn't seem that bad. We're not seeing what the miserable employees are seeing. Some people construct their own realities by conjuring up theories, experiences, and interpretations to which no one else can relate. For those people, getting a new job may not work. Wherever you go, there will be some people who are not a fit. From an organizational point of view, I encourage leaders to identify the degree of fit that exists across the enterprise and take action to strengthen it where possible.

# ONBOARD YOUR SUPERSTARS SO THEY FEEL WELCOME

When new people come aboard, leadership has the opportunity to develop the relationship correctly. Effective leaders must comprehend how to onboard and acclimate newcomers to the organization. With this skill, they can quickly move new employees from being enterprise outsiders to enterprise insiders so they feel well taken care of and have a soft landing instead of a rough start. Everyone responds positively to being eased into a new situation.

For example, the first several days of employment would ideally consist of the new team member getting a realistic preview of the job, including meeting coworkers, exploring the environment, learning about the organization's mission, discussing work assignments, and receiving an overview of policies and rules. These first days will set the stage for whether or not new team members are positioned to be their best, do great things, and have meaningful success within the organization.

Ask people what skills they want to develop and what their time frame is for that development. Take an interest in their career path and what's important to them. Give them job variety and job autonomy at appropriate levels. Partner employees with someone senior or someone experienced in an area they're not. Have people teach someone else something that they want to learn. We learn from the process of teaching it to someone else more than we ever will by studying it. It's a great shortcut to development.

Put employees in charge of a part of the organization or project that they are personally skeptical about. Of course, you can't do that too often and you should be careful of the person. Modeling the behavior and attitude you expect goes a tremendous way toward developing talent, even more so when you are explicitly vocal about what you're modeling and why. Finally, you have to put time or money or both against development. Time could be mentoring. It could be assignments where a supervisor spends time with a new hire who is not experienced in an area. It could be training and certification. Have a budget and figure out how to fairly distribute that and leverage it.

## Effective Onboarding

What's really effective is to make sure everything people need to begin their work life shows up on day one when they arrive. If people have a soft landing, you demonstrate that you're paying attention and care enough to make them feel welcome. Anything less than that indicates you don't care and they're just another body for you. Whether it's a soft landing or rough start, it sets the tone. Be proactive and reach out to newcomers before they arrive or as they arrive. It makes a positive impression. One of our colleagues was hired for a new job. When they walked him to his office, it was empty because the boss forgot to order his desk. What kind of impression does that make?

Think ahead about what new employees will need. They have questions and doubts about how things will transpire. Give them a little structure, a preview, and a plan. Part of it depends on the newcomer. Someone with little experience who is right out of school will need more guidance compared to a twenty-year veteran who just needs a little direction and some boundaries. Let newcomers shadow a supervisor or colleague. Let them see how someone else works in a role before you put them in the same or a similar position for their job. It can provide a great opportunity for observation and interaction. Having a leader deliver a part of the new employee orientation is another way to energize people early on.

Some people just seem to be fabulous at what they do. One woman comes to mind. Those around her are amazed at how wonderful she is, but no one is willing to see how much energy her boss invested to help her become a superstar. It takes a lot of work to make people superstars in your organization. They don't typically show up that way. People learn something when they are given a job assignment, shadow somebody, or watch high performers in action. Most important, people learn something when they want to learn something and when they make a conscious decision to be coachable.

How do you hire for what's coachable? One way is to look for self-efficacy, which is the inner drive to achieve a desired result. This quality is different from self-esteem. For example, people can come from highly dysfunctional homes and lack self-esteem. In spite of this lack of self-esteem, they put themselves through college, receive their first job offer, and earn high-performance ratings and promotions. It wasn't because mom, dad, or someone else encouraged them. It was their internal drive to do whatever it takes, or "self-efficacy," that created their coachability. The key to acclimating newcomers is immersion in a job experience that uses the person's strengths, married with the opportunity to see expertise modeled by high performers. It's incumbent on the organization to provide information and people to go to for help. Supervisors or managers should encourage newcomers to seek out help and answers, to write down questions, and to come see them. Supervisors should also appoint a mentor to get them squared away.

## Turning Ineffective Onboarding into Success

A new person came to one of our client organizations as a government employee in the area of acquisition. He was hired onto the team during a time of very active hiring. Acquisition in the federal government is a very challenging profession. There are a ton of things to know, a new language to learn, and it take years to understand half of what people are talking about, especially with so many acronyms. He had no government experience when they brought him on and put him on a team. He wasn't doing anything because he didn't know how to do anything. He developed a bad reputation for not doing anything, because he didn't have anything to do; and he didn't have anything to do because he didn't know how to do it.

His supervisors moved him to another team, and he did nothing. Then, they moved him to a third team. One of our consultants was coaching the leader of the third team, and he said he had heard negative things about this low-performing individual and didn't know what he could do. Our consultant said, "I've heard the same things, but I'm not sure anyone has really given him a chance. My advice is to keep him by your side and explain everything to him as it's happening until you can figure out what he'll be able to do."

So that's what the third supervisor did. It was a huge investment of time. It took about a year, but the employee is on his own two feet now. Now, he talks on and on about the boss who helped him so much and how incredibly grateful he is to him. This is one person in a unique situation, but the takeaway is that you have to put in the time with the people you hire. You can't expect to bring people on without an investment on your part. You can't expect to have no relationship with them. You can't expect them to be perfect. You may have to help with things you assumed they would already know how to do. You have to personally commit to their success.

## Research Shows Great Onboarding Builds Success

The body of scientific knowledge about onboarding indicates that it is critical to employee performance. Following are some interesting research studies that support this assertion.

### Impact on turnover

In one study, turnover was shown to be highest for new employees and to pose problems for organizations because they did not recoup investments made in recruitment and selection. One of the primary drivers in newcomer turnover is inadequate socialization. "Successful socialization is the transformation from outsider to participating and effective insider." Socialization tactics are "methods organizations use to help newcomers adapt." An example is providing newcomers with "common learning experiences such as with a group or cohort," versus exposing each newcomer to learning experiences individually. All socialization tactics looked at in this study were significantly positively correlated with on-the-job embeddedness.[13] When I think back to losing Vivian, this research indicates that we could have socialized her much more effectively to help her create optimal fit in her new job.

### Importance of leadership

Leader-member exchange (LMX) theory "proposes that leaders form unique relationships with each of their subordinates so that high-LMX employees receive greater growth opportunities and higher levels of support" than low-LMX employees. In one study, for introverts, high LMX was positively related to job performance and negatively related to turnover intentions. Employees who were introverts with high LMX relationships experienced higher gains in performance and lower intentions to withdraw. The probability of remaining with the organization (the survival function) for individuals was higher for high-LMX introvert employees.[14] For employees who are introverts, it can be very important for leaders to form unique relationships with them. Again, in hindsight, Vivian was an introvert, and I expect that stronger support from and interaction with her supervisor might have influenced her to stay rather than quit.

### Honeymoon and hangover

The honeymoon-hangover effect is interesting. Here's how it works. First, low satisfaction precedes a voluntary job change. An increase in job satisfaction immediately follows the job change because people want to think positively and commit to the new job. This is the honeymoon. Over time, job satisfaction declines. The positive reactions taper as the employee settles into the job and the organization. This is the hangover.

Wendy R. Boswell, John W. Boudreau, and Jan Tichy suggest "understanding the nature of the honeymoon-hangover effect can help employers retain highly valued individuals, such as high performers, by allowing the employer to anticipate initial euphoria and subsequent tapering off. Employers can intervene to help high performers understand that the tapering off is an expected and typical reaction rather than a signal that they should leave." Also, "organizations can avoid overreacting to subsequent attitude reductions."[15] Given that job satisfaction eventually tapers off, it is worthwhile to consider attitude when selecting employees. If I had known about the honeymoon-hangover effect at the time I hired Vivian, I would have made sure that we discussed it with her so that she understood the phenomenon and how it might affect her thoughts and feelings about her job and the organization.

### Pre-entry perceptions

The degree to which newcomers perceive how their own job-related skills and abilities fit with the skill and ability requirements that are conveyed to them during organizational socialization is called pre-entry person-job fit (P-J fit). Research shows that as pre-entry P-J fit perceptions increase, voluntary turnover rates decrease. The degree to which newcomers perceive how their own values fit with the values conveyed to them during organizational socialization is called pre-entry value congruence. As pre-entry value congruence increases, voluntary turnover rates decrease.[16] In the case of Vivian, her perception of value congruence was high when she started her new job, but her perception of person-job fit was unrealistic because her internship experiences didn't give her a realistic job preview.

### Personality and motivation

One study investigated links between dispositional personality traits (neuroticism, extraversion, openness, agreeableness, and conscientiousness), proactive personality, and motivation to learn. Based on findings, there were several implications for selection and training. First, "when hiring for positions that require continuous learning and frequent updating of skills, organizations may wish to target individuals whose personality traits are predictive of motivation to learn." When evaluating the utility of training programs, consider "assessing the extent to which individuals are likely to be self-motivated." Also, "special situational supports (e.g., supervisor and coworker encouragement) could be arranged for those lacking personality characteristics that heighten motivation to learn." Finally, "when resources (i.e., time and money) for comprehensive personality assessments are limited, measuring proactive personality could be a quick and cost effective method for identifying those most likely to be self-motivated toward learning."[17] This is sound advice, and I've found this practice to be helpful in my company and in our client organizations over the years.

### Rapid onboarding

Keith Rollag, Salvatore Parise, and Rob Cross propose that "rapid onboarding"[18] is the key to making new employees productive quickly. The goal is to help newcomers immediately build an informational network with coworkers.

Rollag et al. believe that employers should ditch the informational approach for a relational approach. The informational approach assumes information and awareness about organizational resources will enable newcomers to seek out and obtain what they need to be productive. The relational approach is about helping new hires rapidly establish a broad network of relationships with coworkers that they could tap to obtain the information they need to become productive. Coworkers can help newcomers figure out the real issues that need to be addressed and identify the important people for a particular issue. This also helps people feel more connected to the organization. Reflecting on my experience with Vivian and many other employees over the years, I can see how being aware of these onboarding myths could have helped expedite and enhance the onboarding experience of many individuals.

### More findings and guidance

Finally, Alan Saks, Krista L. Uggersley, and Neil E. Fassina conducted a meta-analysis to examine the relationships among socialization tactics, newcomer adjustment, and moderators such as type of newcomer (e.g., recent graduates). Based on their findings, Saks et al. offer several recommendations. First, provide newcomers ample opportunities to socialize and network with insiders before and after entry. "Newcomers should have frequent opportunities to meet, interact, and work with members of the organization. An increasing number of organizations are initiating social interactions during the recruitment process where future co-workers and senior management are available to meet with potential candidates. Once hired, newcomers should be assigned to senior employees who will act as buddies and mentors." Finally, before investing too much into social tactics, onboarding specialists "should focus first on indicators of adjustment such as role conflict, role ambiguity, and perceptions of fit,"[19] which will subsequently affect other outcomes such as job satisfaction and organizational commitment. The focus here is on reducing newcomer uncertainty and improving perceptions of fit. When we start a new job, don't we all want a smooth landing in a place where we feel that we belong?

## BUILD STRONG COMMITMENTS TO RETAIN YOUR SUPERSTARS

Effective leaders must also know how to create alignment by building strong bidirectional commitments and agreements between employees and employers. By demonstrating this wisdom, regular two-way exchanges about the current reality become part of the culture, and everyone knows what to expect. This is the foundation for uniting and guiding people's collective energy to create results greater than the sum of the parts.

In a study that looked at what HR managers do versus what employees value, Ans De Vos and Annelies Meganck explored both parties' views on retention management from a psychological contract perspective. They stated, "Where organizations declare an intention to be customer-focused and committed to a complementary set of human resource practices, they help define their obligations to the staff. More important, these obligations will come to form part of the psychological contract with employees."[20] Findings show that employee dissatisfaction over psychological contracts can lead to negative employee outcomes (i.e., absenteeism) that are likely to impact customer relations. De Vos and Meganck suggest organizations may be able to mitigate adverse consequences of psychological contract breaches by providing employees with credible explanations of the circumstances that led to the nonfulfillment of those contracts.

Create opportunities for people to grow and develop at a pace that's important to them. One of my colleagues lost a valuable employee a couple of years ago because the business unit he was in was about one year behind where he wanted it to be. If he would've waited a year, my colleague could have created the position for him, but what's important was the employee's timeline. This also plays out in larger organizations. Be transparent about the strategy of the organization, how it's changing, and how everybody is a part of it. You might be surprised at how interested people are in things you don't think they would be. When in doubt, share more and more information.

Where the total compensation package is at least market adequate or adequate plus (doesn't take 95th percentile compensation), social responsibility work can help make people feel even better about being connected to the organization. In a strong community outreach program, there's something for people to get excited about. The pride and excitement that comes with that helps retain people.

Minimize surprises. Don't let people get caught off guard by something you need to implement for the good of the organization. Listen to people. Give them plenty of forums to communicate. You don't have to act on everything they say, but let them feel heard. And if you won't act on something, tell them the truth and why.

Everything you do to attract talent also retains it, but there's an additional element. That is to make sure everything you do is as fair as possible and communicated as thoroughly as possible. Be an organization where employees know they could take any problem they have to whatever level they need to. They're not constrained by their supervisor's reaction, and they can go higher up. They have a sense of control over their destiny. They have degrees of freedom if they have an issue that doesn't get resolved right away.

Do not have arbitrary rules, or if you do, then explain them well. A guy who worked at a state office was responsible for the signs posted near gas station pumps that said something to the effect of "Don't overpump" or "Don't overpump because . . . [something's going to happen]." He said if you explained to people why they shouldn't overpump, they'd be more likely not to overpump, versus just telling them not to overpump. If you explain why people should do something, they're more likely to be compliant. If you have rules, explain how they came to be—in terms of profit, revenue, the law, or whatever the issue is that led you to come up with it. A lot of organizations don't bother to explain why things came to be. If you don't explain to employees why you're constraining them, they don't see how it is relevant or adds value, and they think it's an arbitrary rule to harass or inconvenience them. Instead, choose to overcommunicate.

## Managing Obligations

### What obligations do organizations have to their employees?

Organizations are obligated to treat employees and contractors fairly and create opportunities for all kinds of people to succeed (i.e., fairness in selection/hiring practices). They are obligated to provide access to the tools, people, and information that enable all employees to do their jobs. Other obligations include setting expectations, providing feedback on the degree to which they are met, and a reasonable and fair market-based compensation practice. When you promise people something and are unable to deliver, tell them why you didn't provide it, what you will do to mitigate that, and what the next steps are.

Every enterprise leader has an obligation to keep their word. If leaders need to change anything they said they would do, it's best to make it a priority and talk about it in advance. If something was said and then it didn't happen, people are usually extremely upset about it. You have to realize that it's not what you changed; it's the fact that you changed it.

Kate J. McInnis, John P. Meyer, and Susan Feldman examined the link between employee perceptions of the psychological contract and commitments to the organization. Employees reported stronger commitment when the contract was trust-based, negotiated, collective, broad, equal, and long term. The study provides added detail for employers to evaluate their psychological contracts and insight into the features of a contract that fosters employee commitment—"one based on trust, that considers their personal well-being, and treats them as an equal partner."[21]

Finally, if the employment contract is about to be terminated, be honest about it. If a project is no longer going to be funded, and you're in the know about that, the worst thing you can do is keep that information from employees, holding them "hostage" through lack of transparency. Instead, share what you know, when you know it, creating new ground rules for finding work while currently employed.

### What obligations do employees have to their organizations?

Employees and contractors are obligated to protect proprietary enterprise information and represent the organization in a way that enhances rather than detracts from its reputation. They are obligated to behave professionally in the work environment and opt in to business rhythms and cultural interventions. They are obligated to do the job they were hired to do and manage their agreements.

People also have an obligation to be ethical and perform their work as best they can within reason. They have an obligation to support the cause for which they have signed up when they took the job. If your job is to produce quality widgets, you're obligated to do your best to make sure that happens. Employees and contractors have an obligation not to be disruptive or poisonous, or to bring the organization down. Not every day is a good day, but they should try not to be a hindrance and let that affect other people. People, no matter what job title or level of experience, need to be "coachable." They are obligated to identify how they can contribute more. They are also ethically obligated to speak up and say, "My skill set used to be a fit here, but it does not fit anymore."

If individuals want to create a new position for themselves inside the organization, it is their responsibility to "sell" the idea. They need to articulate a business proposition that says: "Here's the competency gap I can fill for the greater good of the organization." Highly energized, engaged, and committed people consider themselves advocates of every organization they work for. Loyalty becomes a mindset and a choice, which says more about them than it does the past, current, or future employer. When an employee or contractor operates from a mindset of radical personal accountability, living life with no excuses, a shift in consciousness occurs. This individual starts thinking like a leader and starts acting like a cocreator for the organization's future.

### What happens when these obligations are not fulfilled?

Graceful exits for individuals who no longer meet obligations are the way to go. You can try to work with people, cut them some slack, and give feedback and time to improve when they're not meeting obligations. When it becomes clear that things are not improving, there's no point in people staying. Change is hard, but you don't do people any favors by holding on to a miserable situation. There are times when people realize leaving or being fired was the best thing that could've happened. They have the opportunity to move on and make their life better.

There shouldn't be a problem if you have the right leadership style.

If you manage agreements and articulate employment contracts, there should be no surprises. Angeles Arrien, PhD, a social anthropologist, studied indigenous cultures from around the world and came up with the following four principles to establish enduring work relationships and build community:[22]

- Show up and be 100 percent present.

- Pay attention to what has heart and meaning.

- Tell the truth without blame or judgment.

- Be open to outcome, not attached to outcome.

If a leader lives these principles, even in the most complex work system, people will thrive.

### How are issues around obligations resolved?

Manage all agreements and be up front and direct about what's not happening. Issues can only be resolved through directly addressing them in conversation. In an energized enterprise, people are willing to have difficult conversations about unmet obligations.

Issues are going to get resolved only through having an authentic and truthful conversation. That's the path to resolution. Both parties in the conversation may realize they didn't have awareness of what they were doing and how it was being perceived. There are all kinds of things in this conversation that may be eye opening. Having a relationship allows you to have that conversation. As food for thought, what if an employer acted from a position that "firing someone is not an option," and the employee acted from a position that "suing the employer is not an option"? Considering that framework might provide an alternative.

Looking at the big picture, Hao Zhao et al. conducted a meta-analysis on the impact of psychological contract breach on work-related outcomes. Based on their findings, Zhao et al. provide several recommendations to practitioners. "Managers should not provide unrealistic promises during recruitment, socialization, and routine work interactions. Managers can alleviate the negative impact of breach by paying closer attention to employees' emotional states and putting out the 'fire' before negative behaviors occur."[23] Examples include providing counseling programs and explaining reasons for unfulfilled promises. Managers should carefully assess their employees' needs and make sincere efforts at fulfilling their obligations, assuming they are reasonable. Even partial fulfillment may help rebuild people's confidence in management.

## Managing Expectations

### What expectations do employees have of their organizations?

You can distinguish between obligations as basic things companies should fulfill and expectations as going beyond obligations to hopes and wishes. Employees and contractors have an expectation that the whole person and whole life be acknowledged and paid attention to in some way. From their point of view, people expect their compensation package overall is going to increase every year. Whether that's possible or realistic is a different question. They expect they're going to have a job next month, next year, and so on. They expect the organization to be stable enough to offer employment. People expect job enrichment over time. Organizations should minimize surprises that affect employees' lives. Give people as much notice as you possibly can if you think something will go sour in the organization. Most individuals expect their organizations to continue to provide them with employment once they are on board.

People have many basic expectations, such as to work with people that they feel good about and a good boss, and to be well and fairly paid. They expect to have work that they enjoy that reasonably challenges them and to be informed of things that might affect them. They expect that they'll never receive less than they are currently receiving (e.g., cutting pay or benefits). They expect things to increase but nothing to decrease. This is human nature and a sticky economics issue. It must be acknowledged and dealt with honestly in open and direct conversations.

### What expectations do organizations have of their employees?

Over the long haul, organizations expect employees and contractors to give their best effort. People in energized enterprises are creative and innovative and give you more than you thought was possible. They anticipate in support of (AISO) instead of waiting for you to ask for something. Organizations have the expectation that people will accept whatever changes happen to the compensation package and be OK with it—meaning it may stay the same or backtrack a bit.

Organizations expect their people to excel at their jobs. Organizations expect people to be loyal but recognize that a certain percentage will leave. Otherwise, they would not put in place so many procedures and processes. Organizations expect people to do their jobs. Leaders expect their people will not be troublesome for them. They want an honest effort for reasonable time. The best organizations expect people to

- have a good attitude
- be pleasant and helpful
- get along with other people
- be willing to work
- be coachable
- be proactive
- try to further any mission they've taken on
- do things that are not always pleasant or fun (e.g., working a weekend to do a report)
- say "yes" to all requests within reason and with a smile
- be willing to change direction without grumbling
- assume good intentions and keep an open mind

### When or how should these expectations be communicated?

Expectations only work if you declare them ahead of time and get agreement around them. For example, you have to talk up front about enriching career development. Managing all agreements is based on expectation. Am I willing to be counted on to reach that expectation or not? When there's a breakdown, how do we address it? Anything that feels like an expectation must be communicated whenever it comes up and then a process put in place to manage what to do if it has not been met.

Regular two-way communication is required to remind all parties of the current reality. Organizations should do their best to communicate expectations. This could be realized by providing a realistic job preview. Letting people know expectations helps them decide whether they're a good fit for the job.

People are often reluctant to express their expectations. Leaders would do well to pay attention and understand the reality of what their employees and contractors are expecting. Sometimes you can pick it up from satisfaction surveys or complaints you receive. A normal first reaction to complaints, or survey results that aren't positive, is to disagree or dismiss them. However, leaders should keep an open mind because there's wisdom in everything. They should ask themselves, "What are we doing that rubs people the wrong way?" "Are we not honoring expectations that we don't really know about?" Being willing to see it will ensure you will. Lots of people are set in their opinions and don't pick up on what's really happening. Be willing to pick up on clues that your employees give you.

In an empirical assessment, Mark V. Roehling examined differences in conceptualization of psychological contracts based on expectation, obligation, or promise, and whether the differences are meaningful for trust, equity sensitivity, work centrality, and education level. On the employee side, "greater trust in one's employer is associated with higher perceived obligations, expectations, and promises. Employees who trust their employer tend to feel more obligated, expect to do more, and perceive themselves as having promised to do more than those who do not trust their employer." However, on the employer side, it depends on the form used. Expectation and promise-based measures were associated with trust. "Employees who reported that their work had a more central role in their life tended to believe they were more obligated to their employer and that their employer was more obligated to them"[24] than those who viewed work as less central. This effect was similar but smaller for promises, and nonsignificant for expectation.

### How are unmet expectations communicated or resolved?

Leaders have to be open and embracing of feedback, acknowledge that the expectation was unmet and where they fell short, and seek creative exploration of remedies. These are difficult conversations for the initiator and the recipient, but they're the sweaty-palm kind of conversations people have in energized enterprises. Communicate expectations every chance you get. People do not devote enough energy to managing agreements and expectations. If people are constantly disappointed, they will not be energized. Managing expectations can be energizing. You may not always have 100 percent control, but you should always let people know when an expectation can't be met and why. Better leaders are able to acknowledge failure. Focus on meeting or coming as close as you can to meeting expectations, not on fixing blame. Apologize for the outcome and get people to move forward. This is a mark of effective leadership.

## QUESTIONS FOR REFLECTION, DISCUSSION, AND ACTION

1. What are our organization's *challenges* in attracting superstars who are a great fit? What are we doing to address those challenges? How's it working for us?

2. What are our organization's *best practices* for hiring people who are a good fit? What evidence do we have that these practices are effective? Ineffective?

3. What are our organization's *challenges* in onboarding our people once we've hired them? What are we doing to address those challenges? How's it working for us?

4. What are our organization's *best practices* for helping new people feel welcome? What evidence do we have that these practices are effective? Ineffective?

5. What are our organization's *challenges* in making sure our folks are truly committed? What are we doing to address those challenges? How's it working for us?

6. What are our organization's *best practices* for building strong employee commitment? What evidence do we have that these practices are effective? Ineffective?

7. What tools, tips, and techniques shared in this chapter would we like to implement in our organization? What are our next steps?

# NOURISH AND ENERGIZE YOUR TEAM: VALUES, FAIRNESS, AND WELL-BEING

## DR. D'S IMPOSSIBLE BREAKFAST

An exceptional leader's experience solidified my belief in the power of an energized team. I'll call this leader Dr. D. It started when Dr. D, CEO of a successful federal government contracting firm in the defense arena, took a series of classes to enhance his leadership abilities. One of his classes was on a Saturday, and Dr. D and his fellow classmates received their final assignment at 9:00 p.m. that night. There were twenty-four people in the class, and their assignment was to feed ninety homeless people who would be expecting a breakfast at 9:00 a.m. the following morning. They had exactly twelve hours!

Not only did they have limited time, but the instructors also said the class was absolutely prohibited from using any personal resources such as cash, credit cards, or phones. They had nothing to spend and limited ability to communicate with each other. Ninety hungry people were showing up the next morning expecting a delicious breakfast. The assignment was to go out and create it from nothing. Then, the instructors left, and the difficulty of the assignment began to sink in. The twenty-four classmates circled together, and the general feeling was, "How do we do something like this?" No one in the room had ever done anything like this before. It was 9:00 p.m. on a Saturday night. They were tired from a long day in class. What could they do? They were in a strange city and didn't know anybody.

Someone asked: "If we did create a breakfast, what would we need?" The group responded that first, they would need dishes and utensils to cook and serve with. Then, they would need food like bacon, eggs, bread, fruit, milk, butter, and so on. Third, they thought they needed decorations to make it fun. So they divided into three teams, and each had an assignment. None of the teams knew what to do, but at least now they had more clarity. There were eight people on each team. Dr. D was on the team responsible for the food. His group had to get bacon and eggs and bread for ninety people, and they had no resources!

Fortunately, they were in a city where most of the stores stayed open all night. They went to supermarkets. Most turned them away. Some were even rude. However, a few gave them good food. But the entire team was on board because they felt it was an important task to help others, it seemed that they'd been given a fair assignment, and they anticipated a sense of well-being if they accomplished this feat. They went all over the place and eventually got the bacon, eggs, and bread . . . even twelve pies from a bakery. They were amazed they had acquired all the food they needed in just a few hours. When they finished around 2:00 a.m., Dr. D's team had no idea what the other two teams had done. They decided they had to have faith that the other groups had the same energy and creativity and had produced similar results.

Dr. D and his group showed up at the breakfast location the next morning. The other teams showed up on time as well. They fed the ninety people and had a blast doing it! They had balloons, bubbles, streamers, and plenty of food left over. They actually had to figure out where to donate the excess. They fed ninety people from nothing . . . nothing, according to Dr. D, but intention, energy, and teamwork. Would you like the people in your organization to exhibit this kind of energized teamwork and create exceptional results like this every day, even in the face of extreme budget cuts? Is this possible?

Yes, energized teams are possible in government agencies, and three ingredients can provide the fuel: values, fairness, and well-being. When teams feel value alignment, perceive fair treatment, and have a sense of well-being, their energy is boosted to achieve bold goals. When these ingredients are missing, teams become malnourished and the enterprise suffers as a result.

## WHY MANAGING VALUES, FAIRNESS, AND WELL-BEING IS DIFFICULT

Every leader would love to have an organization filled with energized teams that invent and implement ways to boost quality, speed, savings, and innovation. These teams would imagine the impossible and then achieve it on a daily basis. They would be aligned with the organization's values, feel that they and their peers are treated fairly, and have an overall sense of well-being that translates into happiness and productivity. But how do you as a leader ensure value alignment, guarantee fairness, and promote well-being to free your teams to see the possibilities for improvement and seize those opportunities to take your organization to the next level? It isn't easy, and there are many challenges.

### Problems with Aligning Individual Values and Enterprise Values

An unaligned enterprise wastes energy. The process of aligning individual and organizational values is difficult. Associates of an unaligned organization may work hard, but their efforts are inefficient, like the scattered rays of a light bulb. Common direction, energy, vitality, harmony, and spirit cannot emerge in an unaligned environment. Often this is because leaders haven't created and communicated values with which people are willing to align themselves. With little or no alignment, empowerment can result in confusion and disorder. Therefore, it is important to both empower and align people. The challenge is discovering a process that allows people to fully employ personal energy and, at the same time, align with others to create something extraordinary.

## Problems with Handling Perceptions of Fairness

By nature, everybody is emotionally wired to care about fairness. People "compare what they get and how they are treated with what others get and how they are treated." Employees and contractors naturally make comparisons in their pay, benefits, and treatment to others—both inside and outside the organization. When people "believe they are treated unfairly, employee engagement and performance" suffer. If individuals think they are contributing more than their colleagues, but that their colleagues are receiving greater rewards, then those individuals believe they are being treated unfairly. Fairness is a difficult concept to define because everyone's perceptions are different, so what seems fair to one person might seem unfair to another.

People often perceive lack of fairness around decision making relative to promotions, pay, and policies. This may be because personal integrity, leadership visibility, or communication efforts are lacking within the enterprise, or perceptions of unfairness may be inaccurate. "People may not fully understand the value of what they have, or they may have mistaken notions" about how things are really done such as performance appraisals, bonuses, or promotions. "In the absence of information," experts say, "employees will form their own opinions."[1] If not addressed, perceptions of unfairness can lead to bigger problems for the enterprise such as low productivity as well as high absenteeism and turnover.

## Problems with Maintaining People's Well-Being

Employee well-being is a relevant and necessary consideration in the modern workplace. At its basic level, well-being is about personal happiness—feeling good, living safely, and being healthy. But sometimes, work undermines the basic purposes and needs in people's lives, and by extension the lives of their families and loved ones. In this respect, well-being is a hugely significant aspect of people's work and careers. Well-being and stress can impact people's core life needs and have huge implications for the mind, body, and spirit.

Although it's a simple concept, well-being is challenging to manage in the workplace. This is partly because many organizations fail to give employees and contractors the tools they need to maintain their optimal levels of well-being. Then the organization's management doesn't know how to respond properly when well-being plummets. This creates a snowball effect, with stress escalating while motivation and morale take a nosedive. Again, management doesn't know how to react, and performance suffers. As a result, well-being initiatives are fast becoming a major part of management policies in organizations around the world as businesses and government agencies attempt to reduce the losses they are suffering due to absenteeism and turnover of unhappy people.

## MAKE VALUE ALIGNMENT A PRIORITY

Effective leaders must know how to demonstrate their values and honor the values of others as they show respect for people's important beliefs, commitments, and attitudes. By putting this knowledge into action, leaders can maintain a supportive work environment that has people beating down the doors to come to work. This makes attracting, recruiting, and retaining talent much easier, which boosts savings of time, energy, and money.

Alignment begins with understanding the values of the enterprise and requires respecting the values of individuals. Members of aligned enterprises share common values but do not sacrifice their personal interests to the values of the enterprise. An investment in creating alignment enables common direction, energy, vitality, harmony, and spirit to emerge.

### Leveraging Employee Engagement for Competitive Advantage

In one study that used information from the Corporate Leadership Council, engagement was defined as "the extent to which employees commit to something or someone in their organization, how hard they work, and how long they stay as a result of that commitment." Nancy R. Lockwood, the author of the study, asserted "not only does engagement have the potential to significantly affect employee retention, productivity and loyalty, it is also a key link to customer satisfaction, company reputation and overall stakeholder value."[2]

Lockwood shared some interesting examples related to business success: "at the beverage company MolsonCoors, it was found that engaged employees were five times less likely than nonengaged employees to have a safety incident and seven times less likely to have a lost-time safety incident. The average cost of a safety incident for an engaged employee was $63, compared with an average of $392 for a nonengaged employee." Therefore, "the company saved $1,721,760 in safety costs" through employee engagement initiatives. These initiatives also helped them recoup performance-related costs because they found discrepancies between "low- versus high-engagement teams totaling $2,104,823."[3]

This research also identified three levels of employee engagement: First, "*engaged employees* work with passion and feel a profound connection to their company. They drive innovation and move the organization forward." Second, "*not engaged employees* are essentially 'checked out.' They're sleepwalking through their work day, putting time—not energy or passion—into their work." Third, "*actively disengaged employees* aren't just unhappy at work: they're busy acting out their unhappiness. Every day, these workers undermine what their engaged co-workers accomplish."[4]

One recommended action is to "improve career development and performance management systems." An additional suggested action is to "create an inclusive work environment: Provide equal opportunities. Educate the workforce about diversity and inclusion. Broaden the acceptable leadership styles for both women and men." Finally, "address work/life needs. Reduce expectations of very long work hours. Provide role models. Rethink career paths. Support involvement in activities outside of work."[5]

## Aligning Individual and Organizational Values

What do I advise? Leaders must be present and aware of the organization's needs as well as knowing who has the passion and talent to address those needs. Leaders must know enough about personal team members to figure out what they might get excited about doing and what might give them cold feet. Effective leaders involve many people in achieving a goal and engage them in a participative process. This makes implementation easy because it's already apparent who's excited about what because it was their idea. Matching people to initiatives then becomes easy.

It is imperative to know what needs to get done and who is the right person for the job. With the right culture and trust built up, leaders can ask people to sacrifice, and they'll often do it, making short-term sacrifices because leadership has been transparent and kept their long-term interest in mind. This is preferred to the ineffective, but often used, command and control style: "You work for me. This is what I need you to do. Do it now."

Whenever an employee or contractor applies his or her talent to an organizational value, it is a good opportunity to reinforce it. Whenever someone makes a suggestion and it aligns to one of the organization's values (such as integrity), leadership can point that out and say, "Thank you, and it also aligns with our value of integrity." That is a hands-on personal task, because you actually have to talk to people. There will always be some team members that align themselves (you can just tell them what the goals are), but for the other people who maybe aren't in the right job, it takes conversations, and it requires effective leadership.

As an example, a colleague named Bob worked at IBM and ran a big security team. Bob had one employee who was outstanding. He sat down with her for a performance review and asked if she was happy. She said, "I want to be a librarian because I value helping people access the information they need to be successful in achieving their goals." So Bob found her a librarian position. As a core value, IBMers are passionate about building strong, long-lasting relationships, and this value was demonstrated to this employee when Bob showed his strong commitment to her in helping her find a library position within IBM. He made that happen. That's what you have to do. Don't just insist that people align with organizational goals. Mesh their goals with the organization's goals. That's a conversation, a relationship, and an intention on your part. It means you'll have a win-win with each person to figure out the best role for him or her.

## EXERCISE FAIRNESS AND JUSTICE

Effective leaders must know how to exercise fairness and justice by taking actions to create perceptions of fairness and justice throughout the workplace. With this knowledge, leaders can manage procedures not only so they are fair, but also so that people see the outcomes of those procedures (such as promotions, bonuses, or awards) as fair. This is important because when people sense that procedures are unfair, their performance is affected negatively.

### The Sunny Side of Fairness

One study in particular provides an interesting metaphor: "Anyone who has watched children negotiate how to share a piece of cake knows that humans are exquisitely sensitive to fairness. Although economic models of decision making have traditionally assumed that individuals are motivated solely by material utility (e.g., financial payouts) and are not directly affected by social factors such as fairness, there is increasing empirical evidence that fairness does play a role in economic decision making . . . because fair outcomes tend to be more materially desirable for the recipient than unfair outcomes in everyday life, it is difficult to distinguish the desire for fairness from the desire for material gain."[6]

In this research, individuals participated in a design manipulating fairness (fair vs. unfair) and material outcome/offer amount (high vs. low). Results showed that fairness and happiness were positively related. Participants reported greater happiness for fair offers than unfair offers. Also, contempt was negatively related to happiness and fairness. Finally, after controlling for the effect of offer amount, fairness still predicted happiness and contempt.

## Biological Bases of Fairness Perceptions

Biology drives our perceptions of fairness. Results of another experiment showed "unfair procedures evoked greater activation in parts of the brain related to social cognition . . . whereas unfair outcomes evoked greater activation in more emotional areas of the brain." The authors urge "managers to be aware of and attend to process aspects, such as adherence to procedural justice rules, knowing that individuals cognitively evaluate such rules"[7] and ensuring the provision of fair outcomes, knowing that individuals respond emotionally to unfair outcomes.

"Simply communicating performance ratings or pay raise decision amounts and focusing on outcome fairness is inadequate. Managers need to realize the importance of communicating procedural justice rule information and adhering to such rules when conducting performance evaluations and making pay raise decisions in order to mitigate negative cognitive reactions and to stimulate activity in areas related to emotional suppression and rule consideration."[8]

## Determining People's Fairness Judgments and When They Want More

How do people judge fairness? A study about determining how people judge fairness suggests that sometimes "procedural information is straightforward and procedural fairness can be judged directly by whether . . . principles of process fairness have been violated or achieved. However, more frequently, procedural justice judgments are made in situations marked by informational uncertainty where there is incomplete or unclear information about whether fairness is actually occurring."[9] Providing employees with complete and clear information is warranted.

Another study discusses "why, when, and how people's general tendency to desire higher process fairness over lower process fairness may be attenuated, eliminated, or even reversed"[10] and suggests that more is not always better than less. When people are treated fairly (e.g., given a voice in decision making or treated with dignity and respect), they are more likely to infer that they are held in high regard and, as a result, feel better about themselves.

## Organizational Justice, Strategic Alliances, and Employee Silence

Another element people find important is their perception of organizational justice. How do we define justice in organizations? Scientists Adam Barsky and Seth Kaplan conceptualize three different forms of organizational justice[11]:

- **Distributive justice:** Perceived fairness regarding outcomes
- **Procedural justice:** "Perceived fairness of procedures used to make decisions (as opposed to the decision itself)"
- **Interactional justice:** "Perceived fair interpersonal treatment when treated with respect, dignity, truthfulness, and propriety [also referred to as interpersonal justice] and when provided with explanations for the decision [also referred to as informational justice]"

Research scientist Yadong Luo examined effects of distributive, procedural, and interactional justice in the context of strategic alliances. Findings indicated that "establishing and adhering to procedural, distributive, and interactional justice goes a long way in maintaining stability and . . . can contribute to success in strategic alliances."[12]

Another study examined the cross-level effects of procedural justice climate on employee silence. Employee silence refers to the "intentional withholding of critical work-related information by employees from their workgroup members." While employee silence can be helpful in terms of managing information overload, reducing interpersonal conflict, and increasing worker privacy, it is most often viewed as harmful in terms of preventing the surfacing of problems, reducing innovation at work, etc.

Findings indicate that employees "refrained from raising sensitive issues at work when they perceived their supervisors to be of high status. It is likely that [these folks] are especially sensitive to risks involved in speaking up with their concerns in workgroups where high status supervisors are present." This was consistent with a previous study that reported "that over 85 percent of the managers and professionals interviewed admitted to remaining silent about at least some of their work concerns."[13] Therefore, it is important for supervisors (especially those with perceived high status) to exhibit behaviors that show employees they are fair and just in determining processes and decisions.

## Managing Perceptions of Fairness and Justice

What does all of this research tell us? Perceived equity among colleagues is always an issue, even if not it's talked about (e.g., office space, laptop upgrade, compensation, assignments, invitations to network events). These are examples of the thousands of judgments people make all the time about what's fair or unfair. This makes a difference in how they show up and how happy or disgruntled they may be about their jobs.

For example, people might request a raise or an increase in contract scope because they think they are contributing at a level that deserves more pay, or don't think they are being fairly compensated for their work. Their supervisor can share parametric data about where they fall in distribution among peers and let them know that their compensation among peers is more than fair. People may still be unhappy, but the issue of fairness or unfairness has now at least been addressed.

On a personal note, I can think of two former client organizations where the reigning perception was that people were selected for jobs based on who they knew and not based on who had the most technical capability. This negatively impacted people's trust and moods. My consulting team suggested that leaders pay attention to obligations and expectations to mitigate the unfairness people felt about particular issues. This helped the situation significantly.

In the event of a breakdown, people will be more receptive when leaders explain their actions and intentions so long as they have been consistently fair. People may observe the same event, but they're likely to experience it differently and may even disagree on what they witnessed. If people have developed a trusting relationship with leadership over the long run, they are more likely to give each other the benefit of the doubt. If that relationship doesn't exist, people will not give leaders a chance even when they are being fair.

To this point, one of my colleagues shared a story about trust and perceptions of fairness and justice that remains with him after more than thirty years. He was in training to be a frontline supervisor by a well-regarded old-timer named Johnny, and they were discussing the fairness of having to work several weekend shifts in a month. Johnny said, "On paper, I am paid $125 extra because I work weekends. That's not how it used to be though." He had previously been paid a lump sum of $125 for each weekend shift. Another division had previously implemented a regular rotation schedule, which required supervisors to work only one weekend shift per month. All workers received $125 each pay period regardless of whether they worked a weekend or not.

When a new general manager was promoted from the division with the regular rotation schedule, the first thing he changed was compensation for weekend shifts at the other divisions. Instead of paying overtime for each weekend shift, everyone received a $125 raise to compensate for the weekend shift requirement. This was not upsetting for supervisors in the divisions who only worked one weekend shift each month, but for Johnny this was unfair because his division worked weekend shifts more frequently.

Soon after, the general manager received a brand new company car. Johnny said, "He got a new Ford Bronco and paid for it with my weekend shift pay." There was probably no real relationship between Johnny's weekend pay and the new company car. The point is the leader who made the decision to change the salary for a whole class of workers allowed the company to buy a new car for him at practically the same time. This sends the message that only certain people have to sacrifice. These events affected Johnny's attitude.

Johnny continued to perform in his job, but if the division head introduced a new initiative, Johnny would not get energized about it because he did not trust the organization or perceive the leadership group as fair.

Another big area for leaders to think about is promotions. People get promoted, and others question the fairness for various reasons. This relates to procedural justice. It's not that someone's idea was chosen, but that it was considered. This comes up all the time. People want to be considered for promotions and have their ideas considered in decision making.

Some government agencies have moved to a competency alignment model. In this model, not every job can be competed for; leaders can move people into certain jobs based on whether they have the competencies required for the job. People who didn't get considered or receive the opportunity to present themselves for consideration think it's unfair. The supervisors of the people who get snapped away into the new job think it's unfair because they're not notified in advance or given time to protest. The execution of what they're doing is considered unfair.

If how you're doing things is perceived as unfair, then people don't even consider whether the outcome is unfair; they just assume it's unfair. Don't assume just because you are fair that it will be perceived that way.

Finally, let's talk about bias. Some leaders truly believe they are not prejudiced, but they are and they don't even know it. They hire and promote people in their own image. This is not solely a white male phenomenon anymore. Women can favor other women at the expense of men, Asians other Asians, African-Americans other African-Americans, and so on. We have to remember that our goal as leaders is to expand our definition of "winners" to include all people with competency sets and styles different from our own. That means we have to value and trust capability that is different from ours and be willing to broker highly visible career opportunities to these individuals.

Every leader needs to understand there is a price to pay for not valuing diversity. The price is that the talented people you've invested in eventually learn "there is no place for you here." How, then, can we be surprised when they seek opportunities for employment elsewhere?

## ATTEND TO PEOPLE'S WELL-BEING

Knowing how to make people's well-being a priority by supporting work-life balance, health, fitness, and family is one of the marks of an effective leader. With this expertise, leaders are better able to take the right actions to reduce their people's stress and strain and have a happy workplace. As society has evolved over time, more and more people expect and demand a workplace that values the whole person and recognizes that everybody's life is multifaceted and requires balance.

Effective leaders must understand how to maintain a supportive environment where employees are not only safe but are also allowed to bring forth their best efforts and to thrive. By mastering this, leaders are equipped to improve the quality of work life for their employees. For example, in a recent study, exceptional federal leaders "fostered a shared sense of ownership among everyone on their team by clearly communicating the team's purpose, repeatedly soliciting their ideas, and proactively supporting the team through good times and bad. In a risk-averse culture like our federal government, rank-and-file employees need that support and top-line cover"[14] to help maintain their sense of well-being.

### The Influence of Psychological Flexibility on Work Redesign

An experiment looking at psychological flexibility examined call center representatives for a financial services organization in two different locations. One location underwent a work reorganization intervention following the principles of participative action research (the PAR group). The other served as a control group. The PAR group displayed improved employee mental health and reduced absenteeism compared with the control group. "People who had higher levels of psychological flexibility perceived that they had greater levels of job control as a result of the intervention, and it was this greater perception of control that led these people to experience even greater improvements in absence rates and mental health."[15] Frank W. Bond, Paul E. Flaxman, and

David Bunce conclude that interventions increasing job control can be fruit-ful in improving people's mental health and lowering absence rates.

## Positive Social Interactions and the Human Body at Work

As a result of one study, the authors Heaphy and Dutton, argue "positive social interactions build people's physiological resourcefulness [and physi-cal health] by fortifying the cardiovascular, immune, and neuroendocrine systems through immediate and enduring decreases in cardiovascular reac-tivity, strengthened immune responses, and healthier hormonal patterns." This, in turn, promotes quicker recovery from the workday. Recovery is defined as "the process by which an individual's functioning returns to its pre-stressor levels and the experience of strain is reduced."[16] Heaphy and Dutton posit that organizational practices, culture, and leadership influence the physiological resourcefulness of the organization's employees.

## Stress, Performance, and Organizational Support

In another study, Craig J. Wallace et al. predicted that challenge stressors are likely to result in increased performance as a result of positive emotions such as eagerness and confidence, and that hindrance stressors are likely to result in decreased performance as a result of negative emotions such as anxiety and apprehension. Challenge stressors were positively related to performance. Hindrance stressors were negatively related to performance. Organizational support moderated the relationship between challenge stressors and performance, meaning the relationship grew stronger as orga-nizational support increased; however, no moderating effect was found for hindrance stressors. This finding suggests organizational support might not help employees cope with hindrance stressors because they do not see their level of effort as directly related to meeting the demands of hindrance stress-ors. Wallace et al. advise employers to "increase challenges related to one's work and remove hindrances from the workplace."[17]

## The Positive Group Affect Spiral

Research has shown that positive group affect is linked to decreased absenteeism and conflict as well as increased cooperation, task performance, and individual well-being. One experiment showed that the more similar (or homogeneous the level of) group members' positive affect, the more the total group positive affect. Work group positive affect was reciprocally linked to group relationship quality. It was also discovered that charismatic leadership facilitates upward spiraling. "Charismatic leaders arouse followers emotionally, evoking positive affective reactions by communicating an emotionally captivating vision." Individuals' or subgroups' organizational cynicism impairs upward spiraling.

"The presence of subgroups or single group members who induce pronounced negativity in an otherwise positive group . . . may diminish mechanism of affective sharing and affective similarity-attraction." Group organizational emotion norms can facilitate or impair upward spiraling. "Emotion norms . . . may urge employees to either suppress positive affective states and expressions (emphasizing for instance rationality instead of emotionality) or to deliberately experience and express positive feelings." Organizational identity facilitates upward spiraling. "A strong and attractive organizational identity is likely to enhance affective sharing within the respective organization's work groups by motivating the expression of positive affect towards the organization."[18]

## Balancing Productivity and Well-Being

Given the research, how do I suggest that leaders move forward? Organizations that choose to hold themselves responsible for employee well-being are more likely to attract and retain enlightened individuals compared with organizations that don't. When people feel good about themselves and their contributions, they'll want to stick around.

Leaders have significant influence in the design of work. I encourage all leaders to design work that doesn't overtax employees to the point that it causes physical or mental harm. Looking back in history, Frederick Winslow Taylor's original work *Principles of Scientific Management* (1911) was written during a time when the workforce was largely unskilled. Organizations were hiring people to do physical labor and getting inconsistent results. Taylor found the inconsistencies stemmed from the design of the work. By redesigning work, he saw a substantial improvement in productivity, perhaps double, finding the employees were less tired at the end of the day. This helped employees produce more output and expend less energy by using better tools and methods, as well as avoiding busywork or work that was not of value. It also reinforced the desired behavior by giving employees additional pay if they continued to follow the new instructions. If they continued to do work the old way, they did not receive more pay.

Reduce waste and reduce rework. Reducing waste and rework reduces stress. If people don't have to spend as much time to get their work done, you put them in a better position to be productive and balanced. Give people tools that won't frustrate them. Information technology tools are often a source of frustration at work. Anything that has to be done more than once is not good for productivity. Design work and tools so tasks can be done right the first time. Error-proof things. Make things so they can only be done the right way, or understand that someone will likely figure out how to do them the wrong way. Avoid asking anything you don't have to ask. Avoid asking for things more than once.

Productivity does not increase with the number of hours worked. There will be a cost when you push people too hard and that will ultimately cost the organization. Effective leaders understand that. Those who continue to push harder are not concerned about turnover. The most powerful message is to have senior leaders model behaviors that concurrently embrace wellness and productivity.

Leaders can destroy employee well-being. Organizations can set up performance bars that are impossible to achieve or organizational constraints that are impossible to overcome. Consider the dilemma of most residents in medical schools throughout the United States. It's not unusual for a physician in residence to work forty-eight hours without sleep. Over time, the result is poor decisions that affect patient care. Employees need to feel that they can safely set boundaries related to their capacity to perform, communicate them to their supervisors, and not feel they will be punished for setting these boundaries.

Effective leaders show an interest in people. This interest doesn't have to be limited to work goals. If a person wants to learn about something that's not under their job description, there should be some flexibility between the supervisor and employee to figure out a way to integrate those personal interests with the job in a way that benefits the company. Even if you can't figure out a way to work it into the job description, at least you've demonstrated the interest. People feel better when they feel respected and treated as a whole person.

For example, a supervisor may present an individual with an award that recognizes the person and the person's family. Or they may tell a personal story about him or her. Considering the person as more than an employee shows that leader's holistic mindset. You might recognize an employee who worked eighty hours in a particular week to meet a deadline. That's a lot for the employee and the family. It's nice to thank them for the sacrifice and to communicate how much they've contributed to the greater good in getting the enterprise where it needs to go. In the end, doesn't everybody want to contribute to the greater good?

## QUESTIONS FOR REFLECTION, DISCUSSION, AND ACTION

1.  What are our organization's *challenges* in creating employee value alignment? What are we doing to address those challenges? How's it working for us?

2.  What are our organization's *best practices* for creating value alignment? What evidence do we have that these practices are effective? Ineffective?

3.  What are our organization's *challenges* in ensuring that people have perceptions of fairness at work? What are we doing to address those challenges? How's it working for us?

4.  What are our organization's *best practices* for ensuring that fairness prevails? What evidence do we have that these practices are effective? Ineffective?

5.  What are our organization's *challenges* in making sure we boost our folks' health, happiness, and well-being? What are we doing to address those challenges? How's it working for us?

6.  What are our organization's *best practices* for strengthening health, happiness, and well-being? What evidence do we have that these practices are effective? Ineffective?

7.  What tools, tips, and techniques shared in this chapter would we like to implement in our organization? What are our next steps?

# LIFT YOUR WORKPLACE TO NEW HEIGHTS: COMMUNICATION, RELATIONSHIPS, AND MOTIVATION

## TRANSFORMING RON'S ENTERPRISE

Ron was the associate commissioner of the Social Security Administration at a time when the federal government, including Social Security, was undergoing extensive cuts and downsizing. In his role as leader, one thing in Ron's domain of responsibility was a production line in which information was gathered by one person and passed on to others for processing. If the information came back indicating that something was wrong with the input, someone would have to find the folder and restart the process. Information was all on paper and moved only as fast as paper could move.

After nine months of little progress on streamlining the process, Ron decided to build a team environment made up of dynamic and effective people throughout the entire organization. In Ron's vision of a healthy team environment, people would support each other, honor their commitments, and communicate openly and honestly while maintaining a positive attitude. In creating this new environment, he empowered people to make the decisions that affected them, and he encouraged one and all to think outside the box. Then, he did something that really grabbed everybody's attention. He challenged his information systems team to build a model field office at the agency's headquarters. He envisioned that this model office would look the same as one of the agency's two thousand field offices but would run much better. He said to his team, "If we're as smart as we think we are, we can demonstrate with this model office how to modernize our field offices to get rid of paper and into a fully online interactive environment to manage big data."

At that time, it could take weeks to get information from databases out in the field because so much data was on paper. A new concept had to be framed and communicated. Ron's team drew up a concept of what a modern environment would look like, and he gave them the go-ahead and committed to providing the resources needed to create the model. But he insisted that his information systems folks at headquarters had to bring in real employees from the field to staff the model office, instead of simply staffing it themselves. The field employees were rotated in and out for a few months at a time, and each new group ran the model office as though it were a real field office. The information systems team used existing applications and showed the rotating employees how they could build and transition to a modern, online, interactive process and system. Amazingly, they accomplished all of this in twelve months.

Next, Ron and his team set up some pilot offices in the field and started to accept electronic applications. For the first application, they had the headquarters employee who oversaw the model office go to York, Pennsylvania, and take the first official application. After the York office was successfully running under the new process, the team built nineteen more, including an office in Washington, DC, which they invited members of Congress and their staffs to come see. When a politician would say, "I want one of these in my district," Ron's team would ask him or her to support the $479 million budget they had submitted to the Hill and would tell the politician that once the budget was approved, there would be one of these offices in his or her district. Due in part to what the politicians actually saw when they visited the new offices, the budget was approved.

What Congress saw was an environment where everyone came out a winner, and everyone was very proud to have been associated with the project. The agency's employees received numerous awards and recognition, and there was a great deal of camaraderie among the people who had made the journey together. In leading his team to transform a government agency, Ron integrated all the functions involved in the administrative system to achieve a new, streamlined approach using cutting-edge technology. He did this by leveraging communication and relationships and by motivating people to achieve a big, bold, and exciting goal.

To create a culture where everybody had an impact, Ron built teams that were focused on an outcome and made sure they all had excellent managers and leaders. People knew they were not just cogs in the wheel. They knew they were not going to get lost. Everything people did contributed directly to the success of the team, and they knew it. This led to a series of successes where everybody on the team felt that his or her performance had a direct impact on overall results. Even though he's had many accomplishments over the years, this is still one of Ron's most treasured success stories.

## WHY COMMUNICATION, RELATIONSHIPS, AND MOTIVATION ARE IMPORTANT AND TRICKY

Would you like to successfully transform your enterprise, even in the face of extreme budget cuts? Is this possible? Yes, transformation is possible in every company and in every government agency, especially when leaders promote and nurture communication, relationships, and motivation. When people communicate effectively, build strong relationships, and are motivated to succeed, the workplace becomes vibrant. When these things are missing, creativity is squelched and innovation disappears. It may seem easier said than done, but if you understand the challenges, you can understand how to overcome them.

Leaders fantasize about organizations full of employees who are chomping at the bit to transform every problem into a solution that results in one success story after another. In such organizations, people imagine the impossible and then make it happen. They communicate effectively, have great working relationships, and are motivated to help the enterprise achieve big, bold goals. But how do you as a leader optimize communication, expand relationships, and ensure motivation that propels your people to roll up their sleeves, jump in, and win the race for enterprise transformation? It isn't always obvious, and the path can be riddled with roadblocks and barriers.

## Challenges with Effective Communication

Common problems in organizations include not communicating enough and not communicating in a timely manner. Why? Often, leaders don't appreciate what people want, so they fail to share information. Subsequently, employees discover what they weren't told when they find it out from someone else. Then, their reaction is, "I wasn't told about this," or "How is this going to affect me? Is it important to me? I wonder what else they're not telling me." Many leaders have strategic and operational issues so figured out from their level that they forget to explain things to people at other levels. Furthermore, when people see that the answer provided to a question is not really an answer, they think there's no sense in asking a question because they won't get a direct answer anyway. For example, when politicians are asked a question they often turn the conversation over to something they want to talk about and ignore the question. People get very frustrated with politicians when they do that, and they get frustrated when their leaders do that too. It's demoralizing and causes people to become apathetic and withdraw. Leadership's challenge on the communication front involves managing what is relayed within an organization—the choice is motivation and transformation *or* fear and hesitation.

## Challenges with Working Relationships

Relationships are like networks, carrying the energy, expertise, and information that can uplift entire organizations to new levels of success. Alternatively, they can create in-groups and out-groups, which sometimes have negative consequences. Relationships can blind people to things they're not able to see about each other because they're friends. People may not be as honest with feedback as they should because they're friends. The perception of playing favorites is another risk to watch out for with friendships. For leaders, it can be difficult to balance professional and personal relationships. When you're a leader you don't get to have the same kinds of relationships with people that you did before you were a leader, and that becomes more evident the higher up you go. Leaders must be aware of whom they're talking to, how much they can say, and what perceptions people have of them. It's lonely at the top. If you don't realize that, you can make a lot of mistakes. What you could say before you can't always say now. Relationships at all organizational levels, from peer friendships to leader-member engagements, come with their challenges.

## Challenges in Motivating People

Motivation challenges become apparent when, for example, goals are not reached, there is high turnover, or it is difficult to find talent. Motivation challenges become even more apparent during transformation initiatives. When people are part of a transformation, they feel somewhat fearful. Fear is a natural response to letting go of familiar things and trying new ones. Staying motivated during a transformation requires people to embrace change and evolution, but the accompanying upheaval and instability, plus the unknown potential effects, can be frightening. The challenge is not how to stop feeling fear; it's how to keep fear from affecting the motivation to create positive change. However, people are not wired to be motivated by change. Some experts suggest that when a person is forced to change a fundamental belief, his or her brain can undergo the same physiological reactions as the brain of someone who is undergoing torture. Thus, at a certain point, emotion about change can be physiologically the same as fear. When it comes to transformation, fear of failure can hold people back mentally, spiritually, and emotionally. This fear interrupts a natural cycle of learning that limits growth, development, and results. Giving up because they're worn down by the fear of failing keeps millions of people unmotivated and stuck in a rut every day. Leaders can't give up when it comes to doing everything possible to turn people's fear into the kind of motivation that creates results.

## THE NATURE OF COMMUNICATION AT WORK AND HOW TO MAKE IT BETTER

In organizations, communication is the system of sharing information among groups and individuals to facilitate coordination, understanding, and cooperation. Organizational communication is the two-way information exchange "on an organization's mega, macro and micro levels." It's the bidirectional flow of information within an organization's structure. In hierarchical structures, communication is primarily vertical. In flat organizations, communication is mostly horizontal. "Diagonal communication consists of interactions between workers and managers in different teams."[1] Effective leaders must be able to exercise and facilitate impeccable two-way vertical, horizontal, and diagonal communications at all levels throughout the enterprise.

### Understanding Organizational Communication

What is at the core of communication in the workplace? According to scientists Peter Monge and Marshall Scott Poole, "organizational communication, by its very definition, constitutes an intersection, one that exists between the study of human communication and the study of human organization."[2] Notable viewpoints on communication include

- **Cultural perspective:** This perspective suggests "almost all [organizations] exist in social communities or ecologies and are interconnected by various relations and networks that constitute a communication infrastructure."

- **Ecological theory:** This theory asserts that communities and populations of organizations strive to secure resources needed for survival and that communication exchange is an essential mechanism.

- **Organizational discourse perspective:** This perspective is based on the premise that organizations are created and sustained through discourse and defines organizational communication as "the practices of talking and writing" and the resulting artifacts that "are produced, disseminated, and consumed."

## How to Communicate Impeccably

The previous theories and perspectives indicate that the communication front is richly intricate and complex. How have we seen leaders improve communication? In a military program office, communication scores from a culture survey were very high. One of the practices that contributed to improved communication was having regular meetings with senior leaders and subordinates. They were very constructive meetings where subordinates did most of the talking. The leaders listened and asked questions about how they could help. It made everybody more comfortable with bringing problems forward. At those meetings, they celebrated people's accomplishments; this added to the positivity of the meetings.

At the top of the list, in light of this example, interaction is key: If you want to know it, want to hear it, and you're open to it, you'll get the information you want from people. If you want to hear things as a leader and promote open communication, you can do that by getting out and about to manage by walking around and interacting with people in your organization. Some leaders do this, but it doesn't mean they want to hear anything. Leaders must have the right attitude to really hear what their people are saying.

Leaders must do a lot of listening. Leaders who are the best communicators do a lot of in-depth listening. In meetings, leaders can experiment with standing in silence, insisting that people ask questions and be willing to have dialogue. Do this instead of calling a meeting, spending time on prepared points, asking if anyone has a question, waiting ten seconds, and then dismissing the meeting if no one says anything after ten seconds. Instead, leaders who stand there and wait two or three minutes will discover that someone will take the risk to speak up. The knowledge to be gained from that employee can be well worth the wait.

Once they have established basic habits such as these, leaders can think about experimenting with more advanced methods. Here are a few to consider that will improve the communication front. Establish communication drumbeats where the leader talks to everybody all at once about the state of the organization. Have all-hands meetings several times a year. Send all-hands emails that encourage two-way communication. And remember, effective emails are "just right" like baby bear's porridge: not too hot and not too cold, which typically means short and succinct. Put a messaging system in place that transmits information out to people and absorbs information back. Pulse people periodically to find out what they want to know. Consider implementing electronic suggestion boxes where someone responds to all inputs.

Quarterly performance discussions, weekly meetings, asking questions (e.g., where they need help), and lunch-and-learns can all help. You can be honest with people and have them trust your response when you're direct and explain, "I can only say this much at this time." People will accept this explanation when you can't give them an answer. Finally, create an environment where all employees, including the leader, are continuously seeking feedback to help themselves be more effective. As the old saying goes, we don't know what we don't know about ourselves. The way to find out what we don't know is to solicit open, honest, and direct feedback. With this information, leaders can make choices to be more effective.

## THE ESSENCE OF RELATIONSHIPS AT WORK AND HOW TO IMPROVE THEM

Effective leaders must know how relationships are built because social bonds enhance results, especially in organizations where people and work are interdependent. With this know-how, leaders can help all employees unite their interests and energies so that people feel like, "We're in this together, and we'll do whatever it takes to achieve our goals." With today's enterprise initiatives being so large and complex, no leader can afford to have a workforce that isn't connected, united, or moving in sync.

## Peers Make the Place

How do our coworkers really affect us? According to scientists Dan S. Chiabura and David A. Harrison, coworkers are "a vital part of the social environment at work; they can literally define it."[3] Their study examined the importance of coworkers in the workplace. Antagonistic coworker behaviors were associated with effort reduction, turnover intentions, and actual turnover. Therefore, coworkers may be detrimental by "providing or withholding their own engagement in tasks, being present or absent, and choosing to stay or quit the organization themselves."[4] Findings also indicated that positive coworker behaviors were negatively related to colleagues' role ambiguity, conflict, and overload. Positive coworker actions were also associated with higher satisfaction and job involvement, and organizational commitment. Coworkers may serve as a potentially rich source of help and information.

## Friendships and Turnover

Do our social networks influence how long we actually stick with a job? Social networks specify who speaks with whom in an organization. Peer relationships over time can strengthen into friendships, creating friend networks. To explore this, one notable experiment examined the role of social networks in the employee retention and turnover process. The major argument is that employees located more centrally in their social networks are less likely to leave. Centrality included speaking to many individuals in the group, being in direct contact with many people, and having an influential position. Findings showed that employees who reported having more friends in the workplace were less likely to have departed after three months. Also, the number of friends was a more important predictor than the closeness of the friendship relations when predicting turnover. Thomas Hugh Feeley, Jennie Hwang, and George A. Barnett concluded that "having a number of different support lines is more important than having one or two close friends to lean on" during stressful times. "With different shifts, different hours, and different responsibilities in the workplace, it makes sense that a more flexible and more available network of [friendships and] social support [are] important."[5]

## Social Interactions Affect the Human Body

Can friendships at work improve our health? A fascinating review looked at several different physiological studies that demonstrate how positive social interactions at work have positive effects on human physiology. Cardiovascular studies showed "positive work relationships are associated with decreases in cardiovascular reactivity at work and beyond." Immune studies showed positive work relationships bolstered the alertness and response of the immune system to challenges (e.g., viruses), which improves both short- and long-term health. Neuroendocrine studies showed positive work relationships prompt the release of the hormone oxytocin, contributing to healthier hormone patterns. Cortisol studies showed "positive relationships contribute to more proportional responses to stress and build long-term reserves of health." These findings support "that positive social interactions build people's physiological resourcefulness [and physical health] by fortifying the cardiovascular, immune, and neuroendocrine systems through immediate and enduring decreases in cardiovascular reactivity, strengthened immune responses, and healthier hormonal patterns."[6] This, in turn, promotes quicker recovery from the stress and strain that are brought on by the workday.

## How to Build Strong Relationships

Gallup research shows the number one reason for retention is having at least one good friend at work. Social bonds are absolutely enhancing to the workplace, especially in organizations and careers where people are interdependent. To get work accomplished, you need trust and bonds among people. Friendships can create an environment where people think, "We're in it together, and we'll do whatever it takes to complete our work." Most people want to enjoy what they're doing every day. Friendships and social bonds make work more fun. The first step is to build social bonds among all people in the organization to promote these conversations. To build bonds in your organization, I recommend implementing the seven leadership rules that were illustrated in Chapter 5.

Next, leaders must create professional and personal relationships with people to learn what motivates them, what their goals and values are, and what their priorities are. In that sense, professional and personal become complementary. It is hard for leaders to help employees with balance and development if they are not taking the time to know their employees at some personal and professional level. However, there must be a balance to mitigate an in-group versus out-group effect.

Finally, leaders must continuously work to unite people's energy around common goals and initiatives that align with what they value. Uniting energy in this way throughout the enterprise builds healthy relationships that promote general happiness and job satisfaction.

In my own company, one of the ways I build relationships with all people and unite them around our common goals is to conduct regular happiness checks with all employees. This involves me sitting down with the employee for a couple of hours and enjoying an in-depth conversation during which I use my very best listening skills. As owner and CEO of the company, my purpose in conducting these interviews is to better understand everybody's work experience, help people become more aligned with company strategy, and use what they share with me to lift them up in any way I can. I do this because I value their talent and experience and what they have to offer as a full participant in the company's success. These are some questions that I use to guide the discussions:

- How satisfied are you with your job? Can you tell me what you believe might increase your level of satisfaction?

- How clearly are your job responsibilities defined? Would you like to receive additional communication of expectations and clarification of your responsibilities? If so, can you tell me more about that?

- How much continuous feedback do you receive to help you achieve? Would you like additional feedback and/or additional encouragement? If so, can you tell me more?

- What are your perceptions of the attitudes, relationships, and happiness in your business unit and throughout the company? What changes in attitudes, relationships, and happiness, if any, would you like to see? What could help make that difference?

- Does working at a company with a mobile and sometimes virtual workforce enable your creativity and/or have a beneficial impact on your life? If so, how?

- How does being an employee here compare favorably to other organizations where you may have worked? Unfavorably?

- What is the single most important change you think should be made that would help you flourish as a professional here?

- Is there additional clarity you would like around our strategic plan including vision, mission, guiding principles, values, strategic goals, and tactical objectives?

- Is there anything else you would like to share with me regarding your work experience?

In 2013, my company won the *Washington Business Journal* Best Places to Work Award in the Washington, DC, area. Employee happiness checks were one of the company's cultural practices that contributed to receiving this honor. Every healthy organization must have healthy relationships, and there's no time like the present for leaders to experiment with strengthening connections with their people and encouraging team members to do the same thing in their own social networks.

# THE MEANING OF MOTIVATION AT WORK AND HOW TO BOOST IT FOR EVERYBODY

Effective leaders must comprehend how to motivate people by supporting sustainable achievement of individual and organizational goals. By motivating everyone in this way, leaders are better able to mentor and accelerate people's professional development and alignment with the organization. When it's all said and done, if people aren't growing, their performance wanes and the enterprise suffers.

## Motivation, Organizational Identification, and Well-Being

How do job tasks and identification with one's employer affect work motivation? To investigate this, Jurgen Wegge et al. examined stress with a focus on the motivating potential of the task and organizational identification as predictors of work motivation and well-being. The authors "examine the relationship between objective job characteristics and employees' perceptions of the motivating potentials of their jobs . . . [and] the relationship of organizational identification with work motivation and well-being." Results showed objective working conditions were associated with the motivating potential of work. "High motivating potential of work is linked with high job satisfaction, high organizational citizenship behaviors (OCB), and low turnover intentions. Thus, enhancing work motivation" is a win-win for employees and the organization. "Employees with high organizational identification were more satisfied with their job, engaged in more OCBs, and were less inclined to leave the organization."[7]

## Pro-social and Intrinsic Motivation

Do people who like to help others enable a motivated workplace? Let's explore. Pro-social motivation is the desire to expend effort to benefit other people. A study by Adam M. Grant[8] examined this and hypothesized that pro-social motivation would be more likely to predict persistence, performance, and productivity when intrinsic motivation is experienced in tandem. Findings supported that intrinsic motivation strengthened the relationship between pro-social motivation and the overtime hours that people worked. Intrinsic motivation also strengthened the relationship between pro-social motivation and the performance and productivity of workers. It was suggested that managers tailor selection and socialization practices toward pro-social and intrinsic motivations. Employees who display dispositional tendencies to experience high levels of both motivations are ideal candidates. Moreover, work contexts should be designed to maximize both types of motivation. For example, task significance and empowerment interventions enhance intrinsic motivation, and by providing expanded opportunities to contribute and benefit others, they may simultaneously enhance pro-social motivation.

## Making Breaks Count

Does taking breaks elevate motivation? To answer this, John P. Trougakos and colleagues[9] examined the challenge to employees who must continually regulate their behavior to present the appropriate emotion to customers to see how taking a break allows employees to restore depleted resources. They examined the relationship between workday break activities and emotional experiences as well as positive affective displays. Findings showed breaks were positively related to positive affect, positive emotion, and chores. The more breaks employees took, the more positive emotion they felt and expressed, plus the more productive they were in terms of chores performed. Further, participants who reported experiencing greater positive emotion during their breaks exhibited higher levels of positive affective displays. Breaks predicted positive affective displays independent of positive emotions. Engaging in chores during break was correlated positively with negative affect. Trougakos et al. concluded that how employees use their daily work breaks may be important in determining the emotions they experience while at work. This could have implications for performance following breaks. Results suggest that employees who work through or skip their daily breaks altogether may not immediately reduce their ability to perform or regulate their emotions. However, given the benefits of breaks, employees should be encouraged to engage in some type of rest or recovery activity, which could potentially reduce burnout and emotional exhaustion.

## Charisma and Positive Emotions

Do charismatic leaders energize people? To explore this, Joyce E. Bono and Remus Ilies looked at leaders' positive emotional expressions on the emotional and attitudinal responses of their followers for the purpose of gaining insight into the way that charismatic leaders—whether consciously or unconsciously—use emotion to influence followers. Bono and Ilies surveyed leaders in work settings on charisma and emotional expression. Results showed the two were positively related.[10] Charismatic leadership can elicit positivity in organizations, and I encourage leaders to experiment with being more charismatic to see what result it produces for them and for their people.

## How to Motivate People to Achieve Bold Goals

Where do leaders begin when it comes to strengthening the motivation front? Notice people who offer a contribution. Thanking them after you notice is an even better step. Acting on it is the best thing you can do. Be sure you tell them you acted on it or why you didn't act on it. No matter how bad the idea, you can still thank them. Welcome all contributions, and you'll foster a welcoming climate. If people don't get a response, they're going to stop giving you input, so respond in some way to people's ideas:

- Acknowledge them.
- Thank them.
- Implement the idea and let them know you're implementing it.
- Or let them know why you're not implementing it.

A great example is Dave, one of our Canadian clients, who oversaw warehouses throughout Ontario that supplied products to grocery stores just as Walmart was threatening to move in. The company had to figure out a way to do what they were doing at 30 percent improved efficiency to prevent outsourcing to Walmart. Dave was masterful about communicating a larger story about how everyone in all the warehouses could band together to save the company and drive Walmart out. He prefaced every communication with the heritage and story of the company (e.g., emails, meetings, conversations, etc.). As a result, all employees knew the story and were telling the story.

To create a collective identity around something bigger, like Dave did, goes back to change and the metaphor of a burning platform. In a nutshell, you have to change, or the platform around you will burn and you will have no choice but to change. Whether something positive is pulling you or something negative is pushing you, you have to make the bigger picture or mission your motivation, and you have to be collective in your efforts to achieve it.

My team worked with one group in an agency that handled a lot of billing and processing. The leaders did a good job of identifying the mission of each department and the performance measures that matched those missions. They tracked them over time, then educated and shared this information with everyone so everyone knew how to drive performance in a proactive, nonthreatening way. It raised the level of energy in the workforce. All employees knew how those measures reflected performance to mission, and how what they did each day drove those measures up or down.

People started doing more with less, and they went after the most valuable work. In the past, they had sometimes spent all day doing the wrong things. But afterward, they spent all day on the right things, and they could see an impact on the organization. They understood the significance of their work and got regular feedback on it. Whenever you can provide visibility and feedback so people can see the relationship between what they produced and the organization's performance for customers, it is energizing. These types of scorecards can be informal and energizing for the entire workforce.

Another tip is to keep the highest-level mission in your communications. Even people who are processing financial paperwork should be hearing that what they do contributes to the organization's mission (e.g., saving lives). Everyone is a piece of a bigger picture that should be producing something important. If you can figure out what that is, that's what you talk about. If you're inclusive and not rejecting people while painting a picture of what's important, you'll create a helping culture. The most effective leaders foster a climate of receiving feedback frequently (e.g., climate surveys and 360-degree feedback). The mechanics of how leaders run a meeting are also important (e.g., making sure that one person doesn't dominate the conversation). One of our military clients always polls team members by asking, "Are you in or are you out?" People who are in show thumbs up. People who are out show thumbs down. In a matter of thirty seconds, this leader polls everybody's opinion, people are satisfied that they have been heard, and an issue has come to closure.

As a final illustration, in one organization every meeting was about looking at balance sheets, financial reports, and task completion status. These meetings were all financially driven, and as you might imagine, looking at all that data was not energizing. The CEO drilled everyone on the "whys." For example, he asked why the revenue was lower than the expense during the first quarter. The answer was: "Because we have to spend most of our money up front during the first quarter to reap the benefit of that investment for the rest of the year. The whole isn't in yet." The CEO didn't believe it until the fourth quarter when the whole story became clear, and the organization exceeded all of its targeted goals. Carole's leadership style was in stark comparison to this. When it was her turn to speak at an "all hands" meeting, Carole simply said: "I want to spend my time genuinely thanking everyone here for all you have done." All she did was express her gratitude. You could see tears in the eyes of people who had worked there for five years and never heard "thank you." She put the rest of the leaders to shame. She became the new informal CEO because of the loyalty she gained. She ended up knowing a lot more about what was going on in different departments than her peers because people came to her. When it's all said and done, transformational leaders like Carole attract people and influence them because they understand how to lift communication, relationships, and motivation to new heights in the workplace.

## QUESTIONS FOR REFLECTION, DISCUSSION, AND ACTION

1. What are our organization's *challenges* in ensuring the communication front is effective with respect to bidirectional communication, both horizontally and vertically? What are we doing to address those challenges? How's it working for us?

2. What are our organization's *best practices* for effective bidirectional communication at all levels? What evidence do we have that these practices are effective? Ineffective?

3. What are our organization's *challenges* in maximizing working relationships? What are we doing to address those challenges? How's it working for us?

4. What are our organization's *best practices* for building healthy relationship networks? What evidence do we have that these practices are effective? Ineffective?

5. What are our organization's *challenges* in motivating people to succeed? What are we doing to address those challenges? How's it working for us?

6. What are our organization's *best practices* for helping people find the most motivation in their jobs? What evidence do we have that these practices are effective? Ineffective?

7. What tools, tips, and techniques shared in this chapter would we like to implement in our organization? What are our next steps?

# PART

## 4

# THE FUTURE

# ENHANCE YOUR LEADERSHIP EFFECTIVENESS NOW: ATTRIBUTES, CHOICES, SIGNS, AND RESULTS

## YOU ARE NOW READY TO ENERGIZE YOUR ENTERPRISE

At this point, I will assert that you have the knowledge you need to increase the level of energy in your organization. So, where are you? As a leader, you may be looking for hope and relief from daily stress and ambiguity, and if you're not, you probably know some people who are. Due to many complexities, you may have realized that cause-and-effect relationships are hard to pinpoint and that quick fixes are not apparent.

Furthermore, you understand that complex systems are difficult to lead and manage. You know that poor performance is challenging to address. You see that many people are stretched too thin as a result of budget cuts and staff reductions. You may be finding that new technologies are slow to be adopted and that your organization's productivity isn't as high as desired. You may also have evidence that your employees and contractors are motivated but lack accountability so that productivity suffers. In addition to experiencing accountability problems, productivity issues, and workforce reductions, you (or leaders you know) may also be struggling to manage low performers and to keep high performers motivated.

But at this point, you see all the challenges you're facing as opportunities for effective leadership because you have learned many ways to improve these situations and the human element. Now it's time for you to take advantage of all that knowledge and make the choices that will drive change. Now is the time for you to get in motion and take action. Fortunately, because you are reading this book, you have already learned many valuable ways to transform your organization and further develop your leadership story.

## TAKE CHARGE OF YOUR OWN STORY

We all have a story, and stories are one of the best ways we learn from each other. I've told you a lot of stories in this book about people I've met over the years with the aim that you would learn from them as I have learned from them. Every character in these stories was seeking to discover something new about leadership, and some even took it a step further to apply what they learned and become more effective.

Now it's your turn. You have a leadership story of your own, and I encourage you to take charge of your story in a new way by taking some risks, stepping outside of your comfort zone, and experimenting with some of the tools and techniques that I've shared with you. But before you set out to enhance your story, let's take a stroll down memory lane to review a few of the insights we gained from some of the characters you've met in previous chapters, including Mr. Jones, Ed, George, Ellen, Prince Richard, Vivian, Dr. D, and Ron.

### Mr. Jones's Headache Was Cured

Back to Mr. Jones and his aspirin demand in Chapter 1. His team—Mr. Jones, Berta, Harry, and Randall—taught me a lot about formal and informal leadership. Most important, they modeled for me that improving the workplace requires clarity, commitment, and energy. Improvement also involves ongoing teamwork, appreciation for diversity, and the ability to manage stress. Mr. Jones helped shine a light on the importance of paying attention to the human element in every enterprise, especially federal agencies. Yes, you can lift the people in your organization's workforce to new heights of satisfaction and performance. And if you do, everything (including your own headaches) will get better.

## Ed Achieved Mission Success

Then, there was my friend Ed in Chapter 2. He led the charge to update old processes, strengthen relationships, and drive organizational change. Ed took a long look at his expectations for client service, training, vendor relations, and budget. He built trust, enrolled people, set goals, documented processes, and defined roles. He also established accountability, communicated effectively, measured performance, and championed training. Empowered people became the life force of Ed's workplace, and his team members' effectiveness escalated as they reached peak performance and achieved mission success. Like Ed, you can empower and align your people as you promote their self-awareness, build a stronger workplace community, and inspire true dedication throughout your enterprise.

## George Chooses to Be a Lifelong Learner

Let's go back to the note from George, my previous client, in Chapter 3. George is a truly great and accomplished leader. Not only does his note touch my heart, but it also shows that he's a lifelong learner, like all effective leaders. George's note illustrates for us that now, more than ever, it's important to exponentially magnify our bright stars in the public sector. George validates for me personally that executives face big challenges in federal agencies when he states, "I have come to believe that the most effective endeavors in public service occur when leadership enables and promotes individual fulfillment simultaneously with organization goals—value alignment precedes attitudes, precedes behaviors, grows culture. The most effective experiences and undeniable success require leaders to weave humanity into their work." By putting this book's lessons in motion, you can lead your people more effectively by getting outside your comfort zone and driving meaningful interactions that magnify individual, team, and enterprise performance.

### Ellen's Eureka Moment Led to Great Things

One of my favorite heroines is Ellen in Chapter 4. Ellen inspired her people to start thinking about the entire enterprise, not just about individuals or insulated groups. She helped her people become total systems thinkers, and this resulted in more funding for everybody. Modeling and mentoring were very important to Ellen's success as an effective leader. Learning to appreciate the total system excited Ellen's people, who were motivated by the chance to contribute their smart ideas and do great work. In putting forth their newfound total systems mindset, they made a significant impact across the organization. Ellen also elevated her teams to collaborate around work assignments and to grab the vision and run with it. As a result, her leadership legacy lives on. Like Ellen, you can help your people see the big picture as you think, speak, and act from the heart. In doing so, you will take your workforce and your organization as a whole to the next level of performance.

### Prince Richard Blossomed and So Did His Kingdom

We can't forget Prince Richard in Chapter 5. Once the prince adopted a set of valuable leadership rules, a magical story unfolded. By adjusting his sentiment and mindset, Prince Richard created a shared vision, attended to people's needs, and encouraged everybody to achieve new heights. He became a better steward of his people by applying strategies, closing gaps, and evaluating results throughout the land. The prince became a king who conquered his thoughts and feelings in new ways that made a positive difference for him, his people, and his entire kingdom. By putting simple leadership rules (such as open, honest, and direct communication) into action, you, too, can lift your enterprise to new heights of satisfaction and success as you help your people flourish.

## Losing Vivian Gave Me Insight About Leading People

As I shared in Chapter 6, it was shocking to me when I lost Vivian, one of the most talented superstars I've ever recruited. Vivian had wanted a lot more interaction and stimulation than my employer at the time provided for her. Because her expectations weren't met, Viv walked away. Our organization suffered the loss of a superstar and paid the price to recruit a replacement. However, there was a positive outcome, in that I was enlightened by Viv's exit interview during which I learned that we hadn't paid enough attention to making sure her preferences were a fit with the organization. It was a painful and expensive lesson, but losing Viv helped me become a more effective leader as I stand at the helm of the company I steer today. You can be a more effective leader by ensuring that your people are a great fit for their positions, by onboarding them so they feel as welcome as possible and fully integrated, and by helping them understand and embrace the mission of your enterprise, which enables all individuals to drive the success of something bigger than themselves.

## Dr. D's Impossible Breakfast Was Possible After All

Then, there's Dr. D in Chapter 7. Dr. D and his classmates fed ninety people from nothing . . . nothing, according to Dr. D, but intention, energy, and teamwork. Not only did they feed ninety people, but they also had a blast doing it and had to figure out where to donate the excess. Dr. D and his colleagues exhibited energized teamwork and created exceptional results in the face of no money—the most extreme budget cut of all. We learned that the fuel for this amazing feat came from three ingredients—his team felt value alignment, they perceived fair treatment, and they had a sense of well-being in their situation. Everybody's energy was boosted to achieve and exceed a big, bold goal. You can boost your people's energy to achieve bold goals too, by helping them understand and ultimately align with your organization's values, by treating everyone justly and fairly, by ensuring this behavior permeates your total system, and by taking diligent action to elevate everyone's level of well-being (e.g., to feel better, live more safely, and be healthier).

## Ron's People Achieved Bold Goals and Transformed Their Enterprise

Finally, there's Ron in Chapter 8. Ron knows that when people communicate effectively, build strong relationships, and are motivated to succeed, the workplace becomes vibrant with productivity and vitality. To create a culture where everybody had an impact, Ron built teams that were focused on a specific outcome and made sure they all had excellent managers and leaders. His people knew they were not just cogs in the wheel. They knew they were not going to get lost in the shuffle and that everything they did contributed directly to the success of the team. This led to a series of big successes where everybody on the team understood that his or her performance had a direct impact on the overall results of the enterprise. You can lead this kind of success by communicating impeccably, which requires a lot of listening; by bonding with your people through conversations about what they think and feel; and by encouraging and implementing their ideas to improve the enterprise.

# WHAT YOU HAVE LEARNED AND CAN NOW WEAVE INTO YOUR STORY

Now it's time to apply what you've learned from the stories and research in this book and exponentially magnify your leadership impact. You'll inspire and guide your workforce's untapped potential to reach uncharted crests of performance during these turbulent times and into the future. Your effective leadership will promote high performance at individual, team, and enterprise levels, and boosting all three will be an ultimate achievement. You can quickly and practically put the tools and techniques from this book into action and weave the results into your leadership story. These techniques are used by effective leaders and are now yours to put into practice. Success with these methods requires that you imagine new possibilities and commit to improving individual, team, and enterprise performance. Let's review some key concepts that you can now apply if you haven't done so already.

## Engaging Employees Pays Off

Effective leaders are lifelong learners who continuously seek new knowledge that will help them make a positive difference and achieve meaningful results. In the federal workplace, putting knowledge about effective leadership into motion pays off. For example, implementing knowledge of effective "leadership played a role in the Federal Deposit Insurance Corp.'s rise to first place [among mid-size agencies in job satisfaction and commitment], up from No. 25 just a few years ago."[1] "During the economic crisis that triggered a rash of bank failures," FDIC leadership "doubled down on trying to engage employees," and that effort paid off with increased satisfaction across the enterprise.[2] This is an instance where, with hard work and determination, federal leaders glued their organization together through bidirectional, horizontal, and vertical interactions that were open, honest, direct, and energizing. Because the federal workforce has endured years of budget cuts and spending freezes, one of the most important drivers that you can leverage to increase worker satisfaction, now more than ever, is employee engagement. Engaged employees are not only more productive, but they are also more committed, more satisfied, and more motivated than employees who are not engaged.

## Transformation Requires a Shift in Perspective and Vision

Assuming you are reading this book because you are interested in effective leadership, I would bet that you want to energize your people and help them leverage their imagination and innovation. I would guess that you want to hire and integrate great people who are committed to your mission and who infuse your culture with sizzling vitality. And I would wager that you want to unleash a magic dynamic within your organization as you create solid relationships, powerful communication, and genuine inspiration. Great! But, ultimately, it's about a mindful and conscious shift in perspective and action. You can't just say you're going to be a leader who cares about the human element like so many others have done with so many quick-fix programs that have come and gone. Your shift in perspective must rely upon a powerful vision that includes attending to your workforce. Otherwise, your performance improvement efforts will go nowhere, because enterprise transformation happens when your workforce is committed, satisfied, and motivated. Throughout this book I've encouraged you to create a collective vision with which your people are willing to align themselves, and you have the tools to do it. Successfully transforming your organization to be its very best requires all people to unite their energy around something bigger than themselves. It's up to you to shift your perspective, enhance your vision, and enroll your people to make big things happen.

## Results Require Commitment

If you are committed to going beyond your own limits and want the most for yourself and others, you have the choice to make it happen. Remember, challenging yourself and others to experiment with new behaviors is part of being an effective leader. With the knowledge and tools that I've laid out, you can empower your people to collectively bring about required change or to maintain needed stability, depending upon your situation and what you need to accomplish. Over the past twenty-plus years, I've had the opportunity to witness leaders bring about this kind of change *and* maintain the stability that boosts enterprise-wide quality, speed, savings, and innovation. These results require your commitment. By committing to adjust your sentiment and mindset, you can cocreate a shared vision, attend to your people's needs, and encourage everyone to achieve new heights. As you become a better steward of your workforce, you can apply corrective strategies, close critical gaps, and evaluate desired results on the human capital front. You can conquer how to think and feel in new ways that make a positive difference for you, your people, and your enterprise. As you adjust your sentiment and mindset, I challenge you to go beyond your current capabilities and convince others to push their limits. You can certainly achieve this, and it will be fulfilling.

## People Love Fitting In, Being Engaged, and Committing to Something Bigger

I suspect that you would love for great people to be beating down your doors to come and work with you, stay long-term, and make a meaningful contribution to your organization during their entire tenure. I encourage you to experiment with the best practices that I've shared with you. This includes hiring superstars who are a great fit. It entails onboarding your superstars so they feel welcome. And it requires that you build strong commitments to something bigger to retain your superstars. Creating a stellar culture does not start with pushing others. Effective leadership starts with pushing yourself to become more conscious of your own strengths, weaknesses, and capabilities. Effective leadership means maintaining and managing your courage, clarity, power, and physical limitations in a way that promotes improvement, civility, and wisdom within yourself and your enterprise. It means serving as a role model for others to follow while they commit to something bigger than themselves.

## Communication, Bonds, Motivation, Values, Fairness, Well-Being—Yes!

I imagine that you fantasize from time to time about an organization full of employees who are chomping at the bit to transform every problem into a solution that results in one success story after another. This is possible in your organization if you promote and nurture communication, relationships, and motivation. When your people communicate effectively, build strong relationships, and are motivated to succeed, the workplace becomes vibrant. I encourage you to think about the nature of communication and take action to make it better. I advise you to contemplate the essence of relationships and take steps to improve these bonds. I implore you to consider the meaning of motivation and then get in motion to boost it for everybody in your enterprise. Motivated and energized teams are possible in your organization, no matter how unique your circumstance. Three additional ingredients that can provide the fuel you need are values, fairness, and well-being. When you ensure that your people feel value alignment, perceive fair treatment, and have a sense of well-being, their energy will be boosted to achieve bold goals. Remember to make value alignment a priority in your organization. Exercise fairness and justice with everybody, and attend to your people's well-being.

## FOUR THINGS TO CONSIDER BEFORE YOU TAKE ACTION

Before you set forth to apply the tools and techniques that I've shared with you, I invite you to contemplate and embrace some important character-istics of effective leaders. These characteristics are attributes, choices, signs, and results, and I encourage you to use all of these as benchmarks when you begin to transform your organization and energize your enterprise. It is really up to you to exhibit great *attributes*, make sound *choices*, manifest *signs* of success, and create bold *results*.

### Attributes of Effective Leadership

As shown in previous chapters, effective leadership lies at the core of an energized enterprise. Effective leadership determines if and how your peo-ple contribute to your organization's achievements and how freely they can contribute the best of themselves to a bigger outcome. Regardless of how much expertise and competence are present in your enterprise, it is your leadership that determines how much of that power is tapped and how energetic your people can be. A change in leadership must pre-cede organizational change. A change in leadership relies on improving your effectiveness while inspiring, modeling, driving, and guiding change around you. Some attributes to consider adopting include self-awareness, heart, sensitivity, and persuasiveness.

#### Self-awareness

People are drawn to leaders who are self-aware, and those leaders have a confidence that warrants the trust others place in them. Build your self-awareness by asking others for their insights on what you don't know about yourself. You will become more effective, both personally and professionally.

#### Heart

Transformation must happen in your heart and in your habits, or change will be superficial and old habits will slip back into place when the pressure is high—just when a new and better way of working is most important. Being in touch with your people is not just a nice idea; it is crucial to the daily function and operation of your organization. This understanding enables you to capture the hearts and minds of your people, who will make their best contributions when they're inspired and fully engaged. As the old saying goes, people don't care what you know until they know that you care.

## Sensitivity

Effective leaders can read people, and they realize that it's imperative to listen and see things from other folks' points of view. Listening is only a start. Being aware of the values and emotions of others is crucial for wielding influence. To have a positive impact on others, first sense how they feel and understand their position. This requires your vigilance and conscious flexibility, and you'll need to respond in real time to feedback and to exercise social competence. If you wish to respond effectively to the people in your working environment, cultivate an awareness of what is important to them.

## Persuasiveness

Effective leaders convince their followers to help them lead. This kind of persuasion requires engaging people's hearts and minds. Many strategic decisions are never adopted, are implemented only partially, or are abandoned at the outset. When ideas are dictated, the result is often failure. But when executives first confer with colleagues to rethink their long-term priorities, plans are more likely to be adopted. You can persuade by collaboration and by exercising patience while people make their own decisions on the basis of full information. As essential steps in influencing others, take the time to establish bonds, collaborate, and be patient.

## Choices of Effective Leadership

Research examining the characteristics of innovative federal leaders to determine their common leadership traits reveals that they demonstrate "great resilience and vision" and are "all able to network and collaborate effectively across stovepipes within their agency and across sectors."[3] This is a result of making the choice to focus your heart and mind on adopting a discipline that will energize your people and help them do more than just work hard. Your discipline will help them go above and beyond with common direction, energy, vitality, harmony, and spirit. Following are some choices you can make as part of adopting a stronger discipline.

### Build your relationships

Effective leaders build relationships, and relationships are the core of their networks. New and maturing bonds expand those networks. Leaders who choose to build bonds naturally cultivate and maintain extensive informal networks. Seek out relationships that are mutually beneficial, and then build rapport. Choose to be less protective of your own time and agenda, and accept more requests to help or work cooperatively with others. It's all a balancing act, and I encourage you to balance your own critical work with helping others as you build accounts of goodwill with people across your sphere of influence.

### Unite people and ideas

Make your vision a shared goal. By engaging the hearts of everyone in transformation, you can prepare your folks to share accomplishment, which would not be possible if all or most of them were not motivated by a sense of connection to something bigger. If they are connected to something bigger, they will want to be better colleagues, helpers, mentors, and even leaders themselves. This is a real transformation that will lead to greater levels of performance and a more complete and effective organization on all levels.

### Leverage your networks

Effective leaders build networks, and strong networks require trust. Networks that you build on trust can be the most supportive allies in your efforts to lead people to greatness. There are many advantages to having well-developed networks. Leaders who leverage their networks have an immense time advantage over those who have to use broader, more general sources of information to find answers. It's estimated that for every hour a well-connected individual spends seeking answers through a network, the average person would spend three to five hours gathering the same information. Your network can also help you influence others because your network's endorsement creates added support and credibility for your idea. A network of contacts is crucial personal capital. Among effective leaders, what benefits the individual also benefits the group. The network of contacts you choose is, in fact, a wealth of knowledge, support, and goodwill that you bring to everyone around you. Build good bonds throughout your career and build a leadership network full of people outside of your daily circles who can contribute to a variety of your bold goals and enhance your leadership story.

## Signs of Effective Leadership

Effective leaders plant and cultivate seeds of energy. In an energized enterprise led by an effective leader, we see possibility thinkers who say, "Sure, we can do that!" or "How can we do that?" Their attitudes are, "We've got each other's backs." People offer help when they know you need it or even if they are not sure you need it. They have a high level of self-confidence. They're awake, alive, alert, and open to whatever is going on in the world. They're always wondering what's next. They're never satisfied or content with the status quo. They're thinking about how to move on to better or different. They laugh a lot. They invite their colleagues to do social things. They are other-aware in that they notice that their colleagues are stressed or upset, and offer to listen or help. Titles and formality don't matter that much. There's a clear decision hierarchy, but all ideas are valued.

You can find this energy in people everywhere. You meet them all the time, and you can see they have it. You can choose to find the people who are already awake and help them get brighter and shinier. In turn, your people will in part be a reflection of the attitude, traits, and behaviors that you as a leader display. Be the energy that you wish to see in your organization. Set expectations for what is acceptable. Model a positive attitude and communicate impeccably. People will follow in your footsteps, and you'll notice the signs.

What are some additional signs we see in an organization with effective leadership? People display positive behavior even when no one is around to witness it. Or they will do the right thing even if a supervisor is not peeking over their shoulder. People show general connection or alignment with organizational objectives. They are aligned and energized by a compelling mission. Everybody looks forward to going to work. They're honest about what's working and not working in doing their job. If something is off track, they feel comfortable bringing it forward and trying to get it resolved. They smile. They are excited about what they need to get done. They have fun.

There's more. One of the first things my colleagues and I notice when we're in an energized enterprise with effective leadership at the helm is buzz. You can feel the buzz. There's a higher pace and energy level. People are much more likely to be proactive and do things ahead of time. They offer ideas. There's speed and proactivity that causes them to make things happen. That's how they get more results. Alternatively, it isn't unusual for some people to underperform in any work setting. However, I assert that organizations don't typically create deadwood overnight. In a seminar featuring Dr. W. Edwards Deming more than twenty years ago, a man in the audience asked, "All this sounds good, but what do we do about the deadwood in the company?" Deming replied, "Was the wood dead when you hired it, or did you kill it?" Everyone in the audience got the message. I'm sure you get it too. My point is that effective leaders bring life, vibrance, spirit, and vitality to their people.

There are some people who are determined to add value and have a good life regardless; they just do it. Even if everyone around them is complaining, they're happy, pleasant, and get the job done. What makes them stand apart is perspective and determination. They've chosen to be that way. They have decided the type of experience they want for themselves and for those around them. Those people are excellent role models and naturally fill the shoes of effective leadership. You may have decided to be one of these people. If so, I applaud you. If not, it's never too late to change. You can decide today.

## Results of Effective Leadership

Your employees and contractors will respond positively if you create a shared vision, attend to their needs, and encourage them to achieve new heights. Their positive response will result in a better workplace with higher performance. All of your stakeholders want to see that happen, including your employees, contractors, fellow citizens, and elected politicians.

With insights into effective leadership gained from this book, you can bring your organization into balance by making small investments in human capital that yield big returns in happiness, productivity, effectiveness, and innovation. By uplifting your people and identifying affordable steps toward a faster, smarter, and happier enterprise, you can transform your enterprise into one overflowing with possibilities. People throughout your organization will be asking, "What is possible, and how can we choose to make it possible by seizing the opportunities around us?"

By implementing the guidance I've laid out, you can achieve three things that I assert are critical to enterprise performance. First, you can successfully use clearly stated goals and focus your efforts to improve performance and let everybody know what you seek to accomplish. As a result of this, your enterprise will operate more effectively as it remains focused on outcomes and measurable goals that clarify priorities and drive performance improvement. Second, you can effectively measure and analyze performance to find which actions work and deserve further investment as well as which do not work and need to be fixed or stopped. Consequently, you can use that information diagnostically to figure out how to improve outcomes and get more value for the funds in your budget. Third, you can even initiate frequent reviews of progress on your goals to monitor trends and identify actions likely to increase performance and reduce costs. This can be your forum to discuss and drive your priorities.

With these three things realized, your enterprise will have changed. It will be an environment where people frequently smile, exhibit happiness, and show an abundance of energy. Any redundancy, waste, and abuse that may exist will be easier to discover, measure, monitor, and eradicate. Your organization will be faster in adopting new and innovative technologies. And you will watch motivated talent remain engaged and productive. Why will this have happened? What will have driven this transformation? You will have driven it as an effective leader. Now what can you do? Awaiting you is a world of opportunity and possibility, which we'll discuss in the final chapter.

## QUESTIONS FOR REFLECTION, DISCUSSION, AND ACTION

1. What am I currently doing to build my self-awareness? How is that working for me? What can I do to become more self-aware?

2. What am I doing to engage my heart in connecting with my people? What else can I do to strengthen my heart connections?

3. How well do I currently read people? What can I do to be a better listener?

4. How would I rate my ability to be persuasive? How can I better exercise collaboration to be more persuasive?

5. What am I currently doing to build strong relationships? How can I be more effective in building bonds?

6. What actions am I currently taking to unite people and ideas? What do I need to do next to become more effective at uniting?

7. How am I building and leveraging my networks? Who is missing from my network, and what am I willing to do to address the void?

8. What great choices am I currently making? What choices do I need to make to be more effective as a leader?

9. What signs and results indicate that I'm an effective leader? What additional signs and results can I choose to create?

10. What is my leadership story?

# IMAGINING POSSIBILITIES FOR GOVERNMENT ENTERPRISES OF TOMORROW

## AN INTERGALACTIC QUEST FOR MISSION SUCCESS

Imagine a parallel universe. In one of its galaxies lives an accomplished and caring leader. His name is Sir Daniel Manchester. Everyone calls him Dan Man for short. Dan Man works hard to make a difference on his planet, Mirth. As a result of his accomplishments, he recently earned a most influential position, Mirth's Supreme Commander of Peace. He now presides over the entire Department of Peace (DoP) enterprise, and his office is housed in a large eight-sided satellite spaceship called The Octagon, which orbits Mirth's atmosphere.

One morning, Dan Man arrives at The Octagon with his head hanging low, having spent his commute reflecting on how much chaos there is within the DoP community. Various departments aren't getting along, nor are they aligned with the DoP vision. Mistakes are happening all around, and some of them are even life-threatening, such as quality control problems with armored space vehicles that are being manufactured to protect troops who travel into deep space on top secret DoP assignments. Dan Man doesn't have information to make decisions that could result in improved enterprise performance or in better conditions for his people. But he realizes that if the DoP's people could be more satisfied and if enterprise performance could turn around, it would be good for peace, and peace equals 100 percent mission success. But before Dan Man can turn things around, he needs a better read on the situation. So he calls on Deputy Sharon Starchaser and asks if she can help discover how the enterprise is performing.

### Sharon Starchaser Seeks to Measure Total Mission Performance

The first person Sharon consults is Mortimer Jones, an expert who provides metrics support to the DoP. Unbeknownst to Sharon, Mortimer has lost interest in measuring performance. His passion is gone. Over the years, he has encountered so much resistance to his ideas that he simply wants to hang on to his job until he turns one hundred (the average lifespan on Mirth is 150) and can comfortably retire.

When Sharon approaches Mortimer, he assures her that he can help. However, he says he will need about a week to do some analyses and pull some charts together. Sharon thinks that seems like a long time. Shouldn't Mortimer have current information about people, processes, and budgets ready at a moment's notice? She needs information now but thinks Mortimer's charts might be worth the wait. She leaves Mortimer's office and sends Dan Man a t-mail (telepathic mail used by high-ranking officials with special brain implants) saying the reports will be done in a week.

A week later, Sharon and Mortimer meet to review the information. He has no evidence whatsoever on what the people of Mirth (the DoP's ultimate customers) think about the DoP's performance. There isn't any information on the millions of DoP employees. Are they satisfied? How are they performing? Do they have unmet needs? Mortimer's information isn't balanced or complete. Sharon has no more sense of how healthy the

DoP is now than she did before meeting with Mortimer. She sends Dan Man a t-mail asking for more time. Dan Man reminds her that his problem is urgent.

## Sharon Escalates Her Search for a Solution to Her Problem

Even though Sharon knows Mortimer is viewed as an expert, she has some doubts about him at this point and decides to call upon Dr. Al Powers for advice. Dr. Al is a leadership guru who does a lot of work with the DoP, but he is usually traveling, helping other less-developed planets. When Sharon reaches Dr. Al, she explains that after meeting with Mortimer she realizes the DoP does not have a comprehensive scorecard for leaders. They simply have a smorgasbord of anecdotes, presentations, tables, and charts that can't help Dan Man, her, or other leaders make sound decisions to improve the DoP or its people's well-being.

Sharon talks with Dr. Al at length about her commitment to this important assignment and to helping improve the DoP's performance. Dr. Al asks, "What do you want? How will you know when you have it? And what are you willing to think, say, and do to get it? Will you start answering those questions in as much detail as you can, Sharon?" Sharon agrees, and Dr. Al tells her he can be at The Octagon in two days, as soon as he returns from travel. Sharon sends Dan Man and Mortimer a t-mail to schedule the meeting with Dr. Al. But Mortimer feels threatened when he receives Sharon's message. Dr. Al anticipates this and contacts Mortimer to schedule a private conversation.

## Open, Honest, and Direct Communication to the Rescue

Two days later, Dr. Al meets with Mortimer in private. Within minutes, Dr. Al is clear about Mortimer's pain and offers these words: "Mortimer, you are holding on to negative stories from your past when you proposed good ideas and they were dismissed. You gave up on yourself and became a victim. But you can choose to believe in yourself again, reassert your power, and be the contributor you want to be. Dan Man and Sharon need your assistance. I know you can help solve their problem."

Later that day, Dr. Al arrives at Dan Man's office for the meeting. Mortimer is nowhere to be seen, but Dr. Al believes in managing all agreements, especially when it comes to time. He lays out his things, and they begin. Sharon and Dan Man ask Dr. Al how to get started. Dr. Al illustrates with some questions. He asks, "Dan Man, as Mirth's Supreme Commander of Peace, what do you want?" Dan Man replies, "I want Peace on Mirth." "What do you mean by that?" Dr. Al inquires. "I mean I want there to be no wars on Mirth," says Dan Man. Again, Dr. Al asks, "What do you mean by that?" Dan Man says, "I want there to be no wars among nations on Mirth, and no wars between Mirth and other planets." "So, you want peace on Mirth, and peace means the absence of war?" "Well, yes, but that's not all." "What else do you want?" Dan Man asserts, "I want citizens of Mirth and all employees of the DoP to feel they have high quality of life and the opportunity to reach their full potential." "What do you mean by . . . ?"

## Energy Makes Things Better!

Suddenly, Mortimer bursts into the room with a flurry of enthusiasm and excitement and says, "I acknowledge that I'm late! But I'm here to tell you I won't rest until together we improve the DoP! I confess I've been coasting for a while now, but an honest friend helped me see how much renewed joy there can be in my life if I choose to experience it, make a difference, and be part of something bigger than myself. So let's get started!"

Yes, Mortimer is energized! And so the dialogue continues, with Mortimer and Dr. Al asking deeper and deeper questions about what Dan Man, Sharon, and the leadership team want to create and what they really mean by "Peace on Mirth." Once Dan Man and Sharon became clear about their priorities, Mortimer guides them toward measuring what they want and building a scorecard for leadership decision making that aligns with total mission success.

## Great Things for Leaders to Know Regarding Their People

With respect to employee performance, the DoP's new metrics include answering the following questions openly, honestly, and directly. How are we doing with respect to the following:

- Hiring superstars who are a great fit?
- Onboarding people so they feel welcome?
- Helping people build strong commitments to the mission?
- Understanding and improving relationships within the DoP?
- Boosting motivation for everybody across the DOP enterprise?
- Making value alignment a priority throughout our organization?
- Exercising fairness and justice with everybody in the enterprise?
- Attending to our people's health, happiness, and well-being?

With these questions being asked and answered on a regular basis by leadership, sound decisions are made to improve the condition of the human element within the DoP. Actions are taken to fix problems and to seize opportunities. One long-term outcome is peace on Mirth. Dan Man receives the Intergalactic Peace Prize. Peace eventually breaks out all over the universe, and everyone lives happily ever after.

We can imagine a parallel universe where enterprises from different planets work together for the greater good of mankind. It may be science fiction, or it may be part of our planet's evolution. Who can say for sure? Maybe this tale isn't so far-out after all. Now, let's step back into the present for a parallel in our own universe, and I'll share with you a story about a very real mission to save thousands of lives.

# HELPING A DEFENSE ENTERPRISE
# ACHIEVE TOTAL MISSION SUCCESS

In October 2006, the US Department of Defense (DoD) Mine Resistant Ambush Protected (MRAP) Vehicle Program (JMVP) Joint Program Office (JPO MRAP) formed. "In May 2007, the JPO's project to procure these trucks became the number-one acquisition priority in the DoD"[1] with demand for MRAP vehicles growing from one thousand to more than fifteen thousand in less than one year. JPO MRAP was tasked with rapidly developing, acquiring, and fielding MRAP vehicles to protect US military personnel in Iraq and Afghanistan from mines and improvised explosive devices.

The MRAP program faced overwhelming challenges, seeking options to implement extremely accelerated fielding plans with a speed not seen since WWII. The program ultimately fielded 28,671 vehicles with a budget exceeding $48 billion. MRAP vehicles averted thousands of injuries and deaths in Iraq and Afghanistan. The Pentagon released statistics that US troops in MRAPs "are as much as 14 times more likely to survive the blast [in MRAPs] than those riding in Humvees."[2]

But rapid expansion and expedited delivery involved growing pains. For example, getting so many employees and contractors hired, integrated, and aligned practically overnight was a huge challenge. Also, as the program hit the ground running, it was sometimes difficult to attend to people's well-being, given the extreme pressure to meet deadlines. Finally, with everything happening so fast, especially during the beginning, it wasn't always easy to ensure impeccable communication. In many cases, the techniques I've shared in this book helped solve these problems.

JPO MRAP had to move quickly and decisively to meet mission-critical needs in a traditionally slow process. The need was critical to improve planning and prioritizing, to codify and streamline processes, to strengthen personnel development and culture, to analyze and rationalize allocation of effort, to assess measurement tools, and to bring together individuals, teams, and processes. In January 2007, a team from my company, Transformation Systems, was tasked with strategic leadership guidance, process analysis and improvement, and management systems engineering solutions. We provided support from program inception through completion of the mission, and in September 2013 we helped facilitate dissolution of the JPO and transfer of the program back to individual DoD Services. Enabling total mission success such as this is the mission of my company.

## Tools and Techniques That Help Clients Accomplish Their Missions

My company's growth has had one source: satisfied customers, including the JPO MRAP, who trust the solutions that are created by our research and development team and executed by talented employees who combine exceptional capabilities, outstanding credentials, and emotional intelligence. These solutions help organizations become leaner, faster, better, and smarter to achieve meaningful and sustainable success. Development and execution of these solutions requires a workforce of energized experts made up of highly credentialed talent—most of our consultants hold PhDs or master's degrees in engineering, business, psychology, and related fields. In addition, most of them have cutting-edge certifications, have worked in both government and commercial sectors, and have spent more than a decade in their area of specialty. All of them know the importance of leading our federal workplaces to new peaks of performance by applying proven tools and techniques to energize the workforce. In the case of JPO MRAP, my team helped this client create results that led to a more productive enterprise and supported mission success.

Our technical approach on JPO MRAP was based on the work of many great applied scientists who came before us. With this approach, our consultants assess where clients are in their improvement process. The consultant then selects the most appropriate consulting mode to help the client move toward success. These modes involve collaboration, analysis, facilitation, coaching, and more. It takes years to master these modes and seamlessly shift from one to the other in response to client needs. With their mastery of the many modes of consulting, our staff applies technical tools such as strategic planning, statistical methods, team-building, process mapping, and human capital management. After applying the tools of our trade and conducting analysis, we convert the results of our analysis into actions. These actions move our clients closer to total mission success, just as you have hopefully moved closer to your own mission success by reading and experimenting with the principles in this book.

### Demonstrating Measurable Value for Enterprise Transformation

The Transformation Systems team supported analysis and decision making for delivery of the first 16,000-plus MRAP vehicles, and the JPO MRAP was able to deliver these vehicles at a pace exceeding the WWII Jeep program and to meet the urgent warfighter requirements. We also drafted the process for evaluating engineering change proposals supporting a $400 million-plus vehicle order decision to provide more maneuverable vehicles to meet specific warfighter needs. One of our Lean Six Sigma Master Black Belts facilitated the improvement of Battle Damage and Repair (BDAR) capability, capacity, and throughput at a vehicle repair facility in Afghanistan. The improvements and new performance baselines were later implemented at two additional repair facilities in Afghanistan, with similar improvements on key metrics and BDAR performance, including cutting repair time in half; doubling service facility capacity; and increasing vehicle/material flow effectiveness/efficiency.

Our team led design, development, and implementation of the JMVP's Enterprise Integration Strategy (EIS) IPT, a team charged with documenting, improving, and aligning Joint, Army, and USMC processes and priorities JMVP-wide. The EIS facilitated process-owner documentation of seventy-plus processes. The EIS peer-review process generated 150-plus process improvement recommendations, most implemented by process owners.

The impact of our team's energy and efforts was significant. We facilitated, consulted, and advised efforts to drive project funding via development and implementation of top priorities. Our team was also able to: select and align health metrics with warfighter priorities; use annual key process review documentation to train and inform users; strengthen linkages among critical retrofit processes; socialize new processes and gather cross-functional feedback via the EIS peer review; and finally, increase sharing of best practices (e.g., safety, packaging, processes).

## Affirmation of Value Added

Our team from Transformation Systems that supported JPO MRAP received numerous certificates and letters from program executive officers, joint program managers, vehicle program managers, and other leaders including:

- Joint Meritorious Unit Award from the joint program manager, MRAP Vehicles. Secretary of Defense Robert Gates awarded government employees of the JPO MRAP with the Joint Meritorious Unit Award for exceptionally meritorious service in support of the US Armed Forces. The joint program manager issued a corresponding citation to our team for contributions to performance that resulted in the Unit Award given the cumulative delivery and support of more than 27,000 vehicles.

- Letter of appreciation from commander, Marine Corps Systems Command, for support of the JPO MRAP Vehicles' fourteen LRIP decisions, tracking thousands of MRAP vehicles and providing expert professional facilitation across the enterprise.

- David Packard Excellence in Acquisition Award, received as contractor member of the Joint Mine Resistant Ambush Protected Vehicle Program team.

- Letter of appreciation from commander, Marine Corps Systems Command, for support of MRAP Vehicle Program LRIP 13 ECP Technical Evaluation Team.

- Letter of appreciation from joint program manager, MRAP, for outstanding contributions and support of Strategic Planning Integrated Product Team.
- Certificates of recognition for leadership of the EIS.
- "Thanks-a-million" certificates from MRAP JPM for support of the EIS IPT.

These awards and recognition are great, and my team and I truly appreciate them. But what we appreciate most is knowing that we help federal leaders who are looking for answers that will ensure their enterprises achieve mission success. We make that happen by bringing to bear and applying the proven tools and techniques of workplace transformation. Not only did we help the JPO MRAP organization in their efforts to drive mission success, but we also helped create similar results within a variety of organizations throughout government and industry. And you can too. It is your choice to seize opportunities and lead the way for your enterprise and its people.

## POSSIBILITIES FOR OUR FUTURE'S VERY BEST GOVERNMENT

In our government's very best future, leaders will have freed people to reach new heights, modeled clarity, engaged everybody, inspired folks to contribute, managed time impeccably, demanded the best information for decision making, and adopted the best disciplines for quality of work life, fairness, relationships, and communication.

Subsequently, the federal workplace of our future will be an environment where people smile, are happy, have energy, and are excited to come to work every day.

Discovering, measuring, and monitoring the evidence of redundancy and waste will be easier. The government will be faster in adopting technologies. The workforce will be motivated, engaged, and filled with people who are alert, growing, thriving, and making a bigger difference. In this new reality, people in the federal workplace will be the special ingredient propelling their agencies to new peaks of mission success.

This new reality will have a positive impact on our nation and throughout the world as our government becomes a benchmark where leaders promote respect among diverse participants and cultivate value alignment enterprise-wide. By encouraging harmony and striking a balance among many stakeholders, federal leaders will become internationally recognized and imitated for integrating everybody to engage one vision with one heart. And these results will be measurable.

While I opened *Energized Enterprise* by talking about the critical need for leaders to foster engagement within their agencies, I will close by taking a look at an imagined intergalactic enterprise where leaders foster engagement by creating a unity of purpose and a harmony among the moving parts that make up all economies and societies. This role is crucial because in our new world reality, a variety of tasks, talents, and personalities are at work. Here, leaders will engage and energize people in a way that is caring, authentic, and effective. They will inspect what's expected and pay close attention to what matters most, the human element.

Tomorrow's most influential national and international leaders will tap into and leverage the power of others to welcome dynamic creativity and encourage openness among all participants on the world scene. This will ensure that cooperation is maximized and all the planet's best talent is guided toward shared goals for the greater good. This is how leaders will transform chaos into peace even as stress escalates around the world.

This transformation will happen when leaders commit to being beacons of energy and inspiration with the intention to make a positive difference. Every leader, including you, possesses the potential to make this commitment. Energy and inspiration will feed the sustainable transformation needed in tomorrow's world environment. Leaders who energize and inspire will, by example, relay their commitment to continuous transformation, and all the elements necessary for a peaceful planet will be present in balance and harmony.

Finally, my experience over the past twenty-plus years of working with leaders in the federal government is that people throughout the government want peace. First and foremost, they want peace within their organizations. The human element is an important component not only of peaceful negotiation but also of peaceful collaboration throughout the government workplace. There can be peace in your workplace and a sense of harmony as you drive toward 100 percent mission success in the day-to-day activities of your agency. By achieving this, you will not only make a positive impact on your immediate sphere of influence, but you can also be part of creating a more peaceful world led by a more focused, effective, efficient, and energized government workforce. Think about it. If we can create a federal workplace that is strong, empowered, connected, and fulfilled, this will inevitably have extraordinary ramifications for the world in general, since what happens in our federal workplace doesn't stay there but reverberates around the world through the thousands of interactions that we have on the world stage.

## QUESTIONS FOR REFLECTION, DISCUSSION, AND ACTION

1. How are we doing with respect to hiring superstars who are a great fit?

2. What results are we achieving with onboarding people so they feel welcome?

3. How are we helping people build strong commitments to the mission?

4. What is our progress with understanding and improving relationships within the organization?

5. What evidence do we have that we are boosting motivation for everybody across the enterprise?

6. How are we making value alignment a priority throughout the workplace?

7. By what method are we exercising fairness and justice with everybody in the total system, and how do we know it is working?

8. How are we attending to our people's health, happiness, and well-being? What impact are we having?

9. What would 100 percent mission success look like for our enterprise?

# ENDNOTES

## Part I: The Challenge

### Chapter 1: Government Employees Deserve Attention

1. United States Office of Personnel Management, *2014 Federal Employee Viewpoint Survey Results: Employees Influencing Change* (Washington, DC: United States Office of Personnel Management, 2014), http://www.fedview.opm.gov/2014.

2. Ibid.

3. United States Office of Personnel Management, *2013 Federal Employee Viewpoint Survey Results: Employees Influencing Change* (Washington, DC: United States Office of Personnel Management, 2013), http://www.fedview.opm.gov/2013.

4. United States Government Accountability Office, *Department of Homeland Security: DHS's Efforts to Improve Employee Morale and Fill Senior Leadership Vacancies,* Testimony before the committee on Homeland Security, House of Representatives (Washington, DC: United States Government Accountability Office, released on December 12, 2013), http://www.gao.gov/products /GAO-14-228T.

5. Ibid.

6. Ibid.

7. Eileen Ambrose, "Ranking Agencies by Job Satisfaction," *Baltimore Sun,* November 24, 2012, http://articles.baltimoresun.com/2012-11-24/news/bs-md -federal-morale-20121121_1_job-satisfaction-federal-workers-tsa-employees.

8. Partnership for Public Service, "The Best Places to Work in the Federal Government 2013 Rankings," http://bestplacestowork.org/BPTW/rankings/overall/large.

9. David Weaver, "NASA Named Best Place to Work in Government," NASA News Release, December 13, 2012, http://www.nasa.gov/home/hqnews/2012/dec/HQ_12-433_Best_Places.html.

10. Wikipedia, "IRS Targeting Controversy," last modified October 5, 2014, http://en.wikipedia.org/wiki/2013_IRS_scandal.

11. Andrew Stiles, "Obama: IRS Targeting 'Intolerable and Inexcusable,'" *National Review Online*, The Corner, May 14, 2013, http://www.nationalreview.com/corner/348331/obama-irs-targeting-intolerable-and-inexcusable.

## Chapter 2: Bright Stars and Black Holes in Government

1. David J. Berteau, Guy Ben-Ari, and Matthew Zlatnik, *Organizing for a Complex World: The Way Ahead* (Washington, DC: Center for Strategic and International Studies, 2009), http://csis.org/publication/organizing-complex-world-way-ahead.

2. Michael Catalini, "Why Is It So Hard to Fire a Low-Performing Government Employee?" *National Journal*, May 24, 2013, http://www.nationaljournal.com/politics/why-is-it-so-hard-to-fire-a-low-performing-government-employee-20130524.

3. Dennis Cauchon, "Some Federal Workers More Likely to Die than Lose Jobs," *USA Today*, updated July 19, 2011, http://usatoday30.usatoday.com/news/washington/2011-07-18-fderal-job-security_n.htm.

4. Catalini, "Why Is It So Hard to Fire a Low-Performing Government Employee?"

5. Emily Long, "Federal Performance Officers Stretched Too Thin, Study Says," *Government Executive*, April 12, 2011, http://www.govexec.com/oversight/2011/04/federal-performance-officers-stretched-too-thin-study-says/33767/.

6. Redshift Research, "Adoption, Approaches & Attitudes: The Future of Cloud Computing in the Public and Private Sectors," June 2011, http://www.amd.com/Documents/Cloud-Adoption-Approaches-and-Attitudes-Research-Report.pdf.

7. Redshift Research, "Adoption, Approaches & Attitudes: The Future of Cloud Computing in the Public and Private Sectors," as cited in Elizabeth Montalbano, "Public Sector Slow to Adopt Cloud Computing," *Information Week*, June 2, 2011, http://www.informationweek.com/government/cloud-saas/public-sector-slow-to-adopt-cloud-comput/229900072

8. Samuel J. Heyman Service to America Medals, Medal Recipients, http://servicetoamericamedals.org/SAM/recipients/sam12.shtml.

9. Samuel J. Heyman Service to America Medals, 2012 Justice and Law Enforcement Medal Recipient, Louis Milione and the Operation Relentless Team, http://servicetoamericamedals.org/SAM/recipients/profiles/jlm12_milione.shtml.

10. Samuel J. Heyman Service to America Medals, 2012 Management Excellence Medal Recipient, Elliott B. Branch, http://servicetoamericamedals.org/SAM /recipients/profiles/mem12_branch.shtml.

11. Samuel J. Heyman Service to America Medals, 2012 National Security and International Affairs Medal Recipient, Charles Scoville, http:// servicetoamericamedals.org/SAM/recipients/profiles/nsiam12_scoville.shtml.

## Chapter 3: Turbulent Waters Threaten Every Enterprise

1. Jerry P. Haensich, "Factors Affecting the Productivity of Government Workers," *SAGE Open*, March 13, 2012, http://intl-sgo.sagepub.com/content/early/2012 /03/05/2158244012441603.full.

2. "Improving Productivity and Performance in Government," *How Gov Leads* (blog), May 13, 2010, http://howgovleads.com/2010/05/13 /improving-productivity-and-performance-in-government/.

3. Deltek, "The 35th Annual Deltek Clarity A&E Study, On-Demand Webinar," produced in collaboration with ACEC, ACEC Canada, and SMPS, http://more.deltek.com/2014-AE-Clarity-Report.

4. Jennifer Liberto and Mike Mount, "Defense Worker Furlough Notices to Go Out Friday," *CNNMoney*, March 19, 2013, http://money.cnn .com/2013/03/19/news/economy/defense-furloughs/index.html.

5. John S. Monroe, "Why Stability Trumps Innovation," *Federal Computer Week*, September 12, 2011, http://fcw.com/articles/2011/09/12/back-talk-federal -employee-survey-innovation.aspx.

6. Tom Fox, "Dealing with Poor Performers in Government," *Washington Post*, April 19, 2013, http://www.washingtonpost.com/national/on-leadership /dealing-with-poor-performers-in-government/2013/04/19/77d58398-a92c -11e2-a8e2-5b98cb59187f_story.html.

7. Andy Medici, "DHS Agency that Secures Federal Buildings Is Failing in Its Mission, GAO Finds," *Federal Times*, September 11, 2012, http:// www.federaltimes.com/article/20120911/FACILITIES02/309110004 /DHS-agency-secures-federal-buildings-failing-its-mission-GAO-finds.

8. Alfonso Kennard, "Federal Hostile Workplace Complaints on the Rise," Kennard Law.com, October 23, 2012, http://www.kennardlaw.com /blog/2012/10/federal-hostile-workplace-complaints-on-the-rise.shtml; Susan Crabtree, "Report: Hostile Work Environment Complaints Up on Capitol Hill," *Washington Post*, October 18, 2012, http://www.washingtontimes.com/blog /inside-politics/2012/oct/18/report-hostile-work-environment-complaints-capitol/.

9. "How Budget Cuts Could Affect You," *CNSNews.com*, February 28, 2013, http://cnsnews.com/news/article/how-budget-cuts-could-affect-you; "How Budget Cuts Could Affect You," AP The Big Story, March 13, 2013, http://www.bigstory.ap.org/article/how-budget-cuts-could-affect-you-11.

## Chapter 4: The Bedrock of Leadership Is the Human Element

1. Leonard A. Schlesinger, Robert G. Eccles, and John J. Gabarro, *Managing Behavior in Organizations* (New York: McGraw-Hill, 1983), 486.

2. Interview with Vaughan Limbrick.

3. Wikipedia, "Approach-Avoidance Conflict," last modified June 12, 2014, http://en.wikipedia.org/wiki/Approach-avoidance_conflict.

## Chapter 5: Leadership Rules and Wisdom to Lift Your People

1. "The Heart Has Its Own 'Brain' and Consciousness," in5d Alternative News, updated September 28, 2014, http://www.in5d.com/heart-has-brain-and-consciousness.html.

2. Wikipedia, "Imagination," last modified October 3, 2014, http://en.wikipedia.org/wiki/Imagination.

3. Michael D. Mumford, "Where Have We Been, Where Are We Going? Taking Stock in Creativity Research," *Creativity Research Journal* 15 (2003): 107–120, http://dx.doi.org/10.1207/S15326934CRJ152&3_01.

4. Wikipedia, "Innovation," last modified November 24, 2014, http://en.wikipedia.org/wiki/Innovation.

# Part III: The Opportunity

## Chapter 6: Engaging Your Superstar Staff: Fit, Onboarding, and Commitment

1. U.S. Department of Labor, "Employee Tenure in 2002" (Washington, DC: Government Printing Office, 2002); and U.S. Department of Labor, "Number of Jobs Held, Labor Market Activity, and Earnings Growth Among Younger Baby Boomers—Results From More Than Two Decades of a Longitudinal Survey" (Washington, DC: Government Printing Office, 2004) as cited in Keith Rollag, Salvatore Parise, and Rob Cross, "Getting New Hires Up to Speed Quickly," *MIT Sloan Management Review* 46.2 (2005): 34–41, http://sloanreview.mit.edu/article/getting-new-hires-up-to-speed-quickly/.

2. R. Williams, "Mellon Learning Curve Research Study" (New York: Mellon Corp., 2003) as cited in Keith Rollag, Salvatore Parise, and Rob Cross, "Getting New Hires Up to Speed Quickly," *MIT Sloan Management Review* 46.2 (2005): 34–41, http://sloanreview.mit.edu/article/getting-new-hires-up-to-speed-quickly/.

3. R. McNatt and L. Light, "Job Turnover Tab," *Business Week* (April 20, 1998): 8, as cited in Keith Rollag, Salvatore Parise, and Rob Cross, "Getting New Hires Up to Speed Quickly," *MIT Sloan Management Review* 46.2 (2005): 34–41, http://sloanreview.mit.edu/article/getting-new-hires-up-to-speed-quickly/.

4. Derek S. Chapman et al., "Applicant Attraction to Organizations and Job Choice: A Meta-Analytic Review of the Correlates of Recruiting Outcomes," *Journal of Applied Psychology* 90.5 (2005): 928–944.

5. Jay Prakash Mulki, Fernando Jaramillo, and William B. Locander, "Emotional Exhaustion and Organizational Deviance: Can the Right Job and a Leader's Style Make a Difference?" *Journal of Business Research* 59.12 (2006): 1222–1230.

6. D. Scott DeRue and Frederick P. Morgeson, "Stability and Change in Person-team and Person-role Fit over Time: The Effects of Growth Satisfaction, Performance, and General Self-efficacy," *Journal of Applied Psychology* 92.5 (2007): 1242–1253.

7. James C. Collins, *Good to Great: Why Some Companies Make the Leap—and Others Don't* (New York: HarperBusiness, 2001).

8. Chien-Cheng Chen and Su-Fen Chiu, "An Integrative Model Linking Supervisor Support and Organizational Citizenship Behavior," *Journal of Business and Psychology* 23.1–2 (2008): 1–10.

9. Amy E. Colbert et al., "CEO Transformational Leadership: The Role of Goal Importance Congruence in Top Management Teams," *Academy of Management Journal* 51.1 (2008). 81–96.

10. Maureen L. Ambrose, Anke Arnaud, and Marshall Schminke, "Individual Moral Development and Ethical Climate: The Influence of Person–Organization Fit on Job Attitudes," *Journal of Business Ethics* 77.3 (2007): 323–333, doi 10.1007/s10551-007-9352-1.

11. Jon Billsberry, "Attracting for Values: An Empirical Study of ASA's Attraction Proposition," *Journal of Managerial Psychology* 22.2 (2007): 132–149.

12. Hilary Anger Elfenbein and Charles A. O'Reilly, "Fitting In: The Effects of Relational Demography and Person-Culture Fit on Group Process and Performance," *Group & Organization Management* 32.1 (2007): 109–142.

13. David G. Allen, "Do Organizational Socialization Tactics Influence Newcomer Embeddedness and Turnover?" *Journal of Management* 32.2 (2006): 237–256.

14. Talya N. Bauer et al., "A Longitudinal Study of the Moderating Role of Extraversion: Leader-member Exchange, Performance, and Turnover during New Executive Development," *Journal of Applied Psychology* 91.2 (2006): 298–310.

15. Wendy R. Boswell, John W. Boudreau, and Jan Tichy, "The Relationship Between Employee Job Change and Job Satisfaction: The Honeymoon-Hangover Effect," *Journal of Applied Psychology* 90.5 (2005): 882–892.

16. Allen, "Do Organizational Socialization Tactics Influence Newcomer Embeddedness and Turnover?" 237–256.

17. Debra A. Major, Jonathan E. Turner, and Thomas D. Fletcher, "Linking Proactive Personality and the Big Five to Motivation to Learn and Development Activity," *Journal of Applied Psychology* 91.4 (2006): 927–935.

18. Rollag, Parise, and Cross, "Getting New Hires Up to Speed Quickly," MIT Sloan Management Review 46.2 (2005): 34–41, http://sloanreview.mit.edu /article/getting-new-hires-up-to-speed-quickly/.

19. Alan M. Saks, Krista L. Uggerslev, and Neil E. Fassina, "Socialization Tactics and Newcomer Adjustment: A Meta-analytic Review and Test of a Model," *Journal of Vocational Behavior* 70.3 (2007): 413–446.

20. Ans De Vos and Annelies Meganck, "What HR Managers Do Versus What Employees Value: Exploring Both Parties' Views on Retention Management from a Psychological Contract Perspective," *Personnel Review* 38.1 (2009): 45–60.

21. Kate J. McInnis, John P. Meyer, and Susan Feldman, "Psychological Contracts and Their Implications for Commitment: A Feature-Based Approach," *Journal of Vocational Behavior* 74.2 (2009): 165–180.

22. Angeles Arrien, *The Four-Fold Way: Walking the Paths of the Warrior, Teacher, Healer, and Visionary* (San Francisco: Harper, 1993).

23. Hao Zhao et al., "The Impact of Psychological Contract Breach on Work-Related Outcomes: A Meta-Analysis," *Personnel Psychology* 60.3 (2007): 647–680.

24. Mark V. Roehling, "An Empirical Assessment of Alternative Conceptualizations of the Psychological Contract Construct: Meaningful Differences or 'Much to do About Nothing'?" *Employee Responsibilities and Rights Journal* 20.4 (2008): 261–290, doi 10.1007/s10672-008-9085-z.

### Chapter 7: Nourish and Energize Your Team: Values, Fairness, and Well-Being

1. Lin Grensing-Pophal, "Addressing Perceptions of Workplace Inequities," *Human Resource Executive Online*, June 17, 2011, http://www.hreonline.com /HRE/view/story.jhtml?id=533339271.

2. Nancy R. Lockwood, "Leveraging Employee Engagement for Competitive Advantage: HR's Strategic Role," *2007 SHRM Research Quarterly* 52.3 (2007): 1–12.

3. Ibid.

4. Ibid.

5. Ibid.

6. Golnaz Tabibnia, Ajay B. Satpute, and Matthew D. Lieberman, "The Sunny Side of Fairness: Preference for Fairness Activates Reward Circuitry (and Disregarding Unfairness Activates Self-Control Circuitry)," *Psychological Science* 19.4 (2008): 339–347.

7. James H. Dulebohn, et al., "The Biological Bases of Unfairness: Neuroimaging Evidence for the Distinctiveness of Procedural and Distributive Justice," *Organizational Behavior and Human Decision Processes* 110.2 (2009): 140–151.

8. Ibid.

9. Steven L. Blader, "What Determines People's Fairness Judgments? Identification and Outcomes Influence Procedural Justice Evaluations Under Uncertainty," *Journal of Experimental Social Psychology* 43.6 (2007): 986–994.

10. Joel Brockner, Batia M. Wiesenfeld, and Kristina A. Diekmann, "Towards a 'Fairer' Conception of Process Fairness: Why, When and How More May Not Always Be Better Than Less," *Academy of Management Annals* 3.1 (2009): 183–216.

11. Adam Barsky and Seth A. Kaplan, "If You Feel Bad, It's Unfair: A Quantitative Synthesis of Affect and Organizational Justice Perceptions," *Journal of Applied Psychology* 92.1 (2007): 286–295.

12. Yadong Luo, "The Independent and Interactive Roles of Procedural, Distributive, and Interactional Justice in Strategic Alliances," *Academy of Management Journal* 50.3 (2007): 644–664.

13. Subrahmaniam Tangirala and Rangaraj Ramanujam, "Employee Silence on Critical Work Issues: The Cross Level Effects of Procedural Justice Climate," *Personnel Psychology* 61.1 (2008): 37–68.

14. Tom Fox, "How to Become a Great Federal Leader Without Senior Leadership Support," *Washington Post*, The Federal Coach (blog), posted June 17, 2011, http://www.washingtonpost.com/blogs/ask-the-fedcoach/post/how-to-become -a-great-federal-leader--without-senior-leadership-support/2011/03/04 /AGGMLxYH_blog.html.

15. Frank W. Bond, Paul E. Flaxman, and David Bunce, "The Influence of Psychological Flexibility on Work Redesign: Mediated Moderation of a Work Reorganization Intervention," *Journal of Applied Psychology* 93.3 (2008): 645–654.

16. Emily D. Heaphy and Jane E. Dutton, "Positive Social Interactions and the Human Body at Work: Linking Organizations and Physiology," *Academy of Management Review* 33.1 (2008): 137–162.

17. Craig J. Wallace, Bryan D. Edwards, Todd Arnold, Lance M. Frazier, and David M. Finch, "Work Stressors, Role-based Performance, and the Moderating Influence of Organizational Support," *Journal of Applied Psychology* 94.1 (2009): 254–262.

18. Frank Walter and Heike Bruch, "The Positive Group Affect Spiral: A Dynamic Model of the Emergence of Positive Affective Similarity in Work Groups," *Journal of Organizational Behavior* 29.2 (2008): 239–261.

## Chapter 8: Lift Your Workplace to New Heights: Communication, Relationships, and Motivation

1. Francine Adams, "Biggest Communications Challenges in Organizations," eHow, http://www.ehow.com/info_8342497_biggest-communications -challenges-organizations.html.

2. Peter Monge and Marshall Scott Poole, "The Evolution of Organizational Communication," *Journal of Communication* 58.4 (2008): 679–692.

3. Dan S. Chiaburu and David A. Harrison, "Do Peers Make the Place? Conceptual Synthesis and Meta-Analysis of Coworker Effects on Perceptions, Attitudes, OCBs, and Performance," *Journal of Applied Psychology* 93.5 (2008): 1082–1103.

4. Ibid.

5. Thomas Hugh Feeley, Jennie Hwang, and George A. Barnett, "Predicting Employee Turnover from Friendship Networks," *Journal of Applied Communication Research* 36.1 (2008): 56–73.

6. Emily D. Heaphy and Jane E. Dutton, "Positive Social Interactions and the Human Body at Work: Linking Organizations and Physiology," *Academy of Management Review* 33.1 (2008): 137–162.

7. Jurgen Wegge, et al., "Work Motivation, Organizational Identification, and Well-Being in Call Centre Work," *Work and Stress*, 20.1 (2006): 60–83.

8. Adam M. Grant, "Does Intrinsic Motivation Fuel the Prosocial Fire? Motivational Synergy in Predicting Persistence, Performance, and Productivity," *Journal of Applied Psychology* 93.1 (2008): 48–58.

9. John P. Trougakos, et al., "Making The Break Count: An Episodic Examination of Recovery Activities, Emotional Experiences, and Positive Affective Displays," *Academy of Management Journal* 51.1 (2008): 131–146.

10. Joyce E. Bono and Remus Ilies, "Charisma, Positive Emotions and Mood Contagion," *Leadership Quarterly* 17.4 (2006): 317–334.

# Part IV: The Future

## Chapter 9: Enhance Your Leadership Effectiveness Now: Attributes, Choices, Signs, and Results

1. Eileen Ambrose, "Ranking Agencies by Job Satisfaction," *Baltimore Sun*, November 24, 2012, http://articles.baltimoresun.com/2012-11-24/news /bs-md-federal-morale-20121121_1_job-satisfaction-federal-workers-tsa -employees; Partnership for Public Service, "The Best Places to Work in the Federal Government," 2013, http://bestplacestowork.org/BPTW/rankings /overall/mid.

2. Ibid.; United States Office of Personnel Management, *2011 Federal Employee Viewpoint Survey Results: Employees Influencing Change* (Washington, DC: United States Office of Personnel Management, 2011), http://www.fedview. opm.gov/2011.

3. Fox, "How to Become a Great Federal Leader Without Senior Leadership Support."

## Chapter 10: Imagining Possibilities for Government Enterprises of Tomorrow

1. David Hansen, Dennis Dean, David Gibson, and Sharon Flinder, "The MRAP Vehicle Project—Project Management Institute Project of the Year Award Nomination," 2013, http://www.pmi.org/learning /project-management-lives-stake-5837.

2. Tom Vanden Brook, "Official Says MRAPs Made the Difference in Wars," *Military Times*, October 1, 2012, http://www .militarytimes.com/article/20121001/NEWS/210010312 /Official-says-MRAPs-made-the-difference-in-wars.

# INDEX

# ABOUT THE AUTHOR

 **Dr. Marta Wilson** has dedicated her career to leadership consultancy while serving as board member, author, catalyst, coach, mentor, researcher, speaker, trainer, volunteer, and fundraiser. She holds a PhD in industrial-organizational psychology, specializing in leadership effectiveness, from Virginia Tech. As founder and CEO of Transformational Systems, Inc. (TSI), she leads TSI's dynamic group of possibility thinkers to help executives achieve bold enterprise transformation goals. For five consecutive years, TSI has ranked on Inc.'s "Fastest Growing Companies in America" list, and the company has also made the prestigious "Virginia's Fantastic 50" list.

The *Washington Business Journal* named Dr. Wilson as one of the twenty-five leading businesswomen in the Washington, DC metropolitan area. Wilson has authored several books including *Everybody's Business: Engaging Your Total Enterprise to Boost Quality, Speed, Savings*, and *Innovation and Leaders in Motion: Winning the Race for Organizational Health, Wealth* and *Creative Power*.

*For more information about Marta,*
*please visit www.martawilson.com.*

# TRANSFORMATION SYSTEMS, INC.

**Founded in 2002** by Dr. Marta Wilson, Transformation Systems, Inc. (TSI) is a woman-owned small business headquartered in Arlington, VA. TSI's scientists and engineers help leaders, their people, and their enterprises to thrive. Clients leverage our customized solutions and extensive expertise in 3 ways:

1. PROGRAMS THAT DEVELOP YOUR WORKFORCE. TSI's presentations, retreats, workshops, and seminars give your employees, managers, and executives valuable insight from science and industry using a combination of experiential learning, individual development, and action planning.

2. ADVISORS WHO CONSULT WITH YOUR RISING STARS. TSI's workplace psychologists and certified coaches help your people heighten their awareness of what it takes to be their best, do great things, and have meaningful success using our unique LEAP Profile and development process to illuminate an improvement path for emerging and experienced leaders.

3. PRACTITIONERS WHO IMPLEMENT IMPROVEMENT. TSI's multidisciplinary consultants help you achieve your goals to boost quality, speed, and savings as well as make your organization leaner, faster, better, and smarter. Our scientists, engineers, and Black Belts use our exclusive PATH planning and QUICK measurement processes to clarify the roadmap to success, motivate accountable individuals, and indicate enterprise performance.

*For more information about TSI, please visit*
*www.transformationsystems.com*